Cromosys Publication

Teach Yourself
HTML5

NIRANJAN JHA SHOWMAN

Founder - Niranjan Jha Showman

+91-9561450045
Learn Advanced Skills
And Get Job Instantly
GERMAN
Python
FRENCH
C++
SPANISH
Java
ENGLISH
HTML5
RUSSIAN
CSS
JavaScript
Cromosys
Education and Technology Research Center
Nallasopara (W), Mumbai

Learn Web Programming
Demo-Class Free
HTML
CSS
React
JavaScript
Typescript
Bootstrap
Cromosys
20 Years of Experience
Nallasopara (W), Mumbai
+91-9561450045

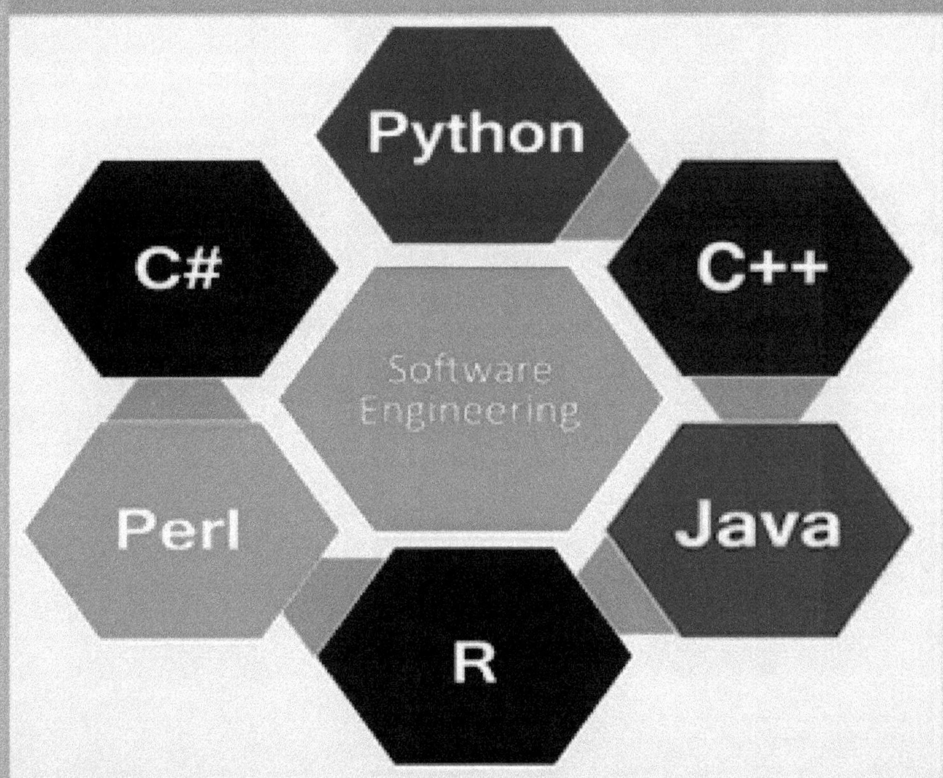

+91-9561450045
Learn Software Engineering
Demo-Class Free
Python
C#
C++
Software Engineering
Perl
Java
R
Cromosys
20 Years of Experience
Nallasopara (W), Mumbai
+91-9561450045

25 Years of Experience
Learn Visual Multimedia
Animation VFX
Movie Editing
Game Development
Cromosys
+91-9561450045
Education and Technology Research Center
Nallasopara (W), Mumbai
www.facebook.com/cromosys

Jobs Available
For Candidates Who Know

German

French

Spanish

Vacancy in Germany, France, Spain

For Hospitality, Engineering, IT Sector
With Free Visa, Airfare and Accommodation

Cromosys

Education and Technology Research Centre
Nallasopara (W), Mumbai
+91-9561450045
20 Years of Experience

+91-9561450045
Foreign Languages Institute
German, French, Spanish
Basic and Advanced - All Levels
3 x 6 = 18 Courses
FRANCHISE
Business Offer
Teaching Materials Provided
We have 1 Million Students Globally
Great Income Assured
Global Exposure
Cromosys
20 Years of Experience
Nallasopara (W), Mumbai
+91-9561450045

Cromosys Publication

Teach Yourself HTML5

Niranjan Jha Showman

"Education taken with zeal educes to success."
~Niranjan Jha Showman

Preface

Cromosys Publication's "Teach Yourself HTML5" book is an optimal quality guide to the beginners and advanced learners. This book is based upon the latest World Wide Web Consortium (W3C) Recommendation of the HTML5.1 specification in the year of 2020. The lessons are written in plain English with simple steps, and all lessons are fully illustrated to help you create web pages instantly. We are the leading book publisher of languages and technology. Our research and education center working from last fifteen years has made tremendous efforts to simplify the learning of HTML5, and so we assure you that this book will walk you through in the simplest way in your entire course of learning, and will make you master of this markup language in just one month of time. This all-inclusive book provides a thorough introduction to the new features of HTML5, such as New Structural Elements, New Form Elements, New Input Types, New Attribute Syntax, HTML5 Graphics, and New Media Elements. It focuses on key features and explains the core concepts of HTML5, a software solution stack that defines the properties and behaviors of web page content by implementing a markup based pattern to it. An easy-to-understand language and step-by-step approach to the concepts that starts from the basics, supplemented with practical examples and its real-time pictures are some of the features that make this book unique. The content is presented in such a way that it will be equally helpful to the beginners as well as the professionals. The lessons conceived and prepared by us help you start learning from real basic making your move amazing, astonishing, and exhilarating for you. It's cool, simple, and sublime!

HTML5 was first released with a major update and W3C Recommendation status in 2014. Its goals were to improve markup language with support for the latest multimedia and other new features. Its goal was also to keep the language easily readable by humans and consistently understood by computers and devices such as web browsers and parsers, and to remain compatible with older software. HTML5 is intended to subsume not only HTML 4, but also XHTML 1 and DOM Level 2 HTML. HTML5 includes detailed processing models to encourage more interoperable implementations. It extends, improves and rationalizes the markup available for documents, and introduces markup and application programming interfaces (API) for complex web applications. For the same reasons, HTML5 is also a candidate for cross-platform mobile applications, because it includes features designed with low-powered devices in mind. The lessons of this book also cover the W3C recommendation. The current specification is known as the HTML Living Standard and is maintained by a consortium of the major browser vendors, such as Apple, Google, Mozilla, Microsoft, and Web Hypertext Application Technology Working Group (WHATWG).

From 2020, you do need to learn its older version such as HTML 4 or XHTML or DHTML because they are obsolete. You just have to focus on HTML5 as the first markup language for Web Development. It includes many new coding features to handle multimedia and graphical content. The new <video>, <audio> and <canvas> elements are added to support vector graphic content, and MathML for mathematical formulas. To enrich the semantic content of documents, new page structure elements such as <main>, <section>, <article>, <header>, <footer>, <aside>, <nav>, and <figure> are added. New attributes are introduced, some elements and attributes have been removed, and others such as <a>, <cite>, and <menu> have been changed, redefined, or standardized. This book is easy to follow, having jargon-free content for fast and productive learning. It covers business and professional skills and all key areas of computing, Internet and digital lifestyle considering the value of your money. Each chapter takes you step-by-step through the functions and uses of a program as every page is packed with visual guides.

HTML5 is the primary language for developing webpages. Let me remind you that if you want to create a professional web page, as per the requirement of your client, then you need to start with web coding in HTML5, and this is why you need to learn HTML5. The online web templates, blogs, Facebook pages or pre-designed applications do not fulfill the professional requirement of clients, so you get into your handwritten coding in HTML5. The creation of this book has been an exciting opportunity for us to discover how the latest specification of HTML5 can be implemented in today's web browsers. It has been fascinating to see how the HTML5.1 specifications are supported in Microsoft Edge, Internet Explorer, Firefox, Google Chrome, Safari, and Opera browsers. The "Handy Reference" section lists the HTML5 tags and attributes that are included in the HTML5.1 specifications. All the examples given in this book demonstrate HTML5 features that are supported by leading web browsers, and the screenshots illustrate the actual results produced by the listed code. We truly believe that now, more than ever, authors can integrate HTML5 content markup, JavaScript functionality, and CSS presentation, to produce stunning interactive web pages.

HyperText Markup Language (HTML) is a modern standard markup language that uses common abbreviations called "tags" to indicate to the web browser how the author would like to have sections of a web page laid out. It was first invented in March 1989 by British physicist Tim Berners-Lee at CERN in Switzerland (the European organization for nuclear research) to share all computer-stored information between the CERN physicists.

As various web browsers were developed, their makers began to add individual proprietary tags – effectively creating their own versions of HTML! For the prevention of this disorder, The World Wide Web Consortium (W3C) came into existence. Berners-Lee created a text browser to transfer information over the internet using hypertext to provide point-and-click navigation. In May 1990, this system was named the World Wide Web, and was enhanced in 1993 when a college student Marc Andreessen added an image tag. Now that HTML could display both text and images, the World Wide Web quickly became hugely popular.

The reason you choose this book because it is the popular introductory guide updated to cover the latest developments for web page design. As you start learning, you will be able to create web pages to display text, images, lists, tables, hyperlinks, forms, audio and video. This book incorporates meta information about a document within 'head' section and how to add structured 'body' content. It teaches you to write script instructions that draw and animate graphics on embedded 'canvas' areas. It also employs key HTML5 APIs and add powerful features to your webpage. This book is ideal for anyone who needs to grasp the latest HTML5 techniques including web developers, students, bloggers, online content writers and enthusiasts eager to enhance their websites. In order to clarify the code listed in the steps given in each example, we have adopted certain colorization conventions.

Niranjan Jha Showman, the author of this and fifty other books published online, is the founder and owner of Cromosys Corporation. His dedication in technological and linguistic research is significantly known to millions of people around the world. This book is the creation of his avowed determination to making HTML5 easy to the students and professional. After you switch on your computer, you just have to follow the instructions of this book doing the same on your computer, and you will see that you are quickly learning everything. Just an hour of practice per day, and in a month of time you will get a lot of knowledge, tips and tricks to work with this markup language. This is an unmatchable unique book of its kind that guarantees your success. The lessons are magnificently powerful to bring you into the arena Web Development. With the industrial growth from the year 2014, the accurate and profound knowledge of HTML5 coding has influenced millions of minds; therefore we conceived the idea of making this book a guideline to those who want to be perfect in this tool starting from real basic. What HTML5 does, no other tool can do. The quick and precise lessons with screenshots will help you enhance your creativity of creating web pages of high-quality designs. It is the need of time and that is why many people have been sharpening their knowledge to be good in this markup language.

Cromosys, our education and technology research center, saving human efforts from being wasted, is dedicated to teach you this subject as good as possible. The world growing with density has brought enormous opportunity to people irrespective of their geographical boundaries. Having been teaching this subject from several years, I have come across numerous unique rules which I have elaborated and explained in this book. Our path-breaking pioneer training institute, Cromosys, is committed to enlightening human mind with educational endeavors, and we are doing the same from fifteen successful years. I believe I have done all that I could to make this book useful to you, and not only hopeful but I am sure that your success is in your hand now because this book will take you miles ahead in your expectation. We always respect the views and comments of readers, so for any communication with regards to assistance, enquiry or collaboration, we are always at your reach as it helps us improve our ability.

Niranjan Jha Showman
Trainer, Author, Journlist, Entrepreneur, Filmmaker, Activist
Founder of Cromosys Corporation
facebook.com/cromosys
notionpress.com/author/814619
+91-9561450045
cromosys@yahoo.com
Nallasopara (W), Mumbai, India

Books by the same author:
Teach Yourself CSS
Teach Yourself JavaScript
Teach Yourself C++ Programming
Teach Yourself Python Programming
Teach Yourself Java Programming
Teach Yourself Autodesk Maya
Teach Yourself Autodesk 3ds Max
Teach Yourself After Effects CS6
Teach Yourself Premiere Pro CS6
Teach Yourself CorelDRAW
Teach Yourself Photoshop CS6
Teach Yourself French
Teach Yourself Spanish
Teach Yourself German

Cromosys Corporation
Education and Technology Research Center
Education, Technology, Publication, Healthcare, Realtor, Filmmaking
facebook.com/cromosys
+91-9561450045
cromosys@yahoo.com
Nallasopara (W), Mumbai, India
Publication date – 2020.

About the Author

Niranjan Jha Showman

Trainer, Author, Journlist, Entrepreneur, Filmmaker, Activist

Niranjan Jha Showman is a Language Scientist and Technical Researcher. He is the Award Winning author of more than fifty educational and fictional books at Amazon. He is one of the great-grandsons of the first President of India Dr. Rajendra Prasad (from adoption). He is a Public Figure, and the globally - renowned Languages Trainer of French, Spanish, and German from past twenty years. Niranjan Jha Showman is an Entrepreneur and also works as a Filmmaker in India. Being the founder and owner of Cromosys Corporation - a company located in Mumbai, India, his company is excelling in the fields of Education, Technology, Publication, Newsmedia, Realtors, Banking, and Cinemascope from past fifteen years.

Niranjan Jha Showman's good-seller educational books and novels are appreciated worldwide. He has more than one million eBook buyers online, and more than one million learners are connected to him globally. Some of his novels is critically acclaimed. He is the trainer of French, Spanish, German, English Voice and Accent, and Advanced Computer Education. He is also a political activist and the founder of Vikaswadi Party in India.

Niranjan Jha Showman is the man who came from rags to riches, he who knows how to turn the table, and he, whom you call the man of Midas-touch, and Renaissance man. He has observed lives from the Pandora of monkeys to the sanctuary of monks, not only down-to-earth but down-to-grave. He is a B. Com. graduate, and B. Ed. from Delhi University, and diploma holder in French, Spanish and German from America. You can watch his songs, movies, educational videos and many more things by typing "Niranjan Jha Showman" in Google.

Niranjan Jha Showman
+91-9561450045
cromosys@yahoo.com
Nallasopara (W), Mumbai, India
www.facebook.com/cromosys
www.notionpress.com/author/814619
www.facebook.com/niranjanshowman
www.facebook.com/vikaswadiparty

Statutory

This book with its content is the registered property of the author Niranjan Jha Showman.
The author and his Cromosys Publication holds all necessary rights of this book.
The copyright certificate of this book is attached at the end of this book.

HTML5 Fundamental

Chapter 1

Introducing HTML5

Welcome to the exciting world of the HTML5 web. This chapter introduces HTML5 and demonstrates how to create a "barebones" valid HTML5 document. Historically, the desire to have text printed in specific formats meant that original manuscripts were "marked up" in red color with annotation to indicate to the book-printer how the author would like sections of text laid out. This annotation had to be concise and needed to be easily understood by both the printer and the author. A series of commonly recognized abbreviations therefore formed the basis of a standard markup language.

HyperText Markup Language (HTML) is a modern standard markup language that uses common abbreviations called "tags" to indicate to the web browser how the author would like to have sections of a web page laid out. It was first invented in March 1989 by British physicist Tim Berners-Lee at CERN in Switzerland (the European organization for nuclear research) to share all computer-stored information between the CERN physicists. Berners-Lee created a text browser to transfer information over the internet using hypertext to provide point-and-click navigation. In May 1990, this system was named the World Wide Web, and was enhanced in 1993 when a college student Marc Andreessen added an image tag. Now that HTML could display both text and images, the World Wide Web quickly became hugely popular.

As various web browsers were developed, their makers began to add individual proprietary tags – effectively creating their own versions of HTML! For the prevention of this disorder, The World Wide Web Consortium (W3C) came into existence. The W3C is the recognized body that oversees the HTML standard and other standards on the web. You can visit their website at www.w3.org. The W3C organization recognized the danger that HTML could become fragmented, so they created a standard specification to which all web browsers should adhere. This successfully encouraged the browser makers to support the standard tags. The W3C's HTML specification was continually revised to introduce new features until the publication of HTML version 4.01 at the turn of the century. At that time the W3C also published a specification for XHTML (eXtensible HTML), which strictly required all code to be "well-formed", to comply with the rules of eXtensible Markup Language (XML). This attempt to coerce web authors into adopting rigorous syntax, as Berners-Lee admits, did not work. So the W3C returned to HTML and finally produced a specification for version 5 in October 2014. This was updated on November 1, 2016 to version 5.1. The supported features of the HTML 5.1 version are described and demonstrated in this book, where it is generically referred to as "HTML5" or just plain "HTML".

1. What's New In HTML5?

Placing great emphasis on backward compatibility, HTML5 is largely a superset of the previous versions, but it introduces some new features that let authors create more meaningful web pages:

- **<main>** - a structural element to contain the main content
- **<article>** - a structural element to contain stand-alone items of content, such as self-contained topic
- **<section>** - a structural element to group together associated content, such as articles related to a common topic
- **<aside>** - a structural element to contain related content
- **<figure>, <figcaption>** - structural element to contain stand-alone illustrations, diagrams, or photos for reference

- **<header>** - a structural element to contain page header content, such as a title, logo, and navigation
- **<footer>** - a structural element to contain page footer content, such as copyright information and contact details
- **<ruby>, <rt>,** and **<rp>** - semantic elements to indicate pronunciation for East Asian languages, such as Japanese
- **<audio>, <video>,** and **<source>** - embedding elements to incorporate audio and video media, such as MP3 music files
- **<embed>** - an embedding element to incorporate media that <u>does</u> require an external plug-in, such as movies in SWF format
- **<canvas>** - an embedding element to create an area in which to dynamically draw bitmap graphics, such as graphs
- **<details>, <summary>** - interactive elements to contain additional information that users can choose to read
- **<menu>, <menuitem>** - elements to add functionality to the web browser's context menu

Drawing on the area provided by the **<canvas>** element is accomplished exclusively using JavaScript and the Canvas 2D API (Application Programming Interface). HTML5 also includes Drag and Drop, Web Storage, and Messaging APIs with which JavaScript can provide dynamic web pages functionality.

- **Tips for you**
  Much effort has been made in HTML5 so that it does not "break the web" – by continuing to define how browsers should deal with legacy markup code.
  HTML5 finally brings intrinsic support for audio and video content with codec support built into the browsers.

Current Web Browsers

Browsers offer varying levels of efficiency, performance, privacy, and security. They differ even more when it comes to unique and helpful features beyond merely displaying websites. W3C has been evaluating web browsers since the dawn of the internet in the late '90s, so we have the expertise to inform your decision. Here, we examine the top five browsers in the US in order of popularity, and provide advice on how to choose the best one for your needs.

Picture 1.1: Current web browsers.

2. History Of Browsers

A web browser is an application through which we can access websites on the World Wide Web (www). It provides users with a medium through which they can interact with a web server as it fetches the data and displays it as a web page. In today's time, there are various web browsers available. Each web browser has some unique characteristics that are distinguished depending on features like speed, security, extensions, etc. Right now, Google Chrome is the most used browser in the world; however, some other popular browsers are being used, like Mozilla Firefox, Opera, Microsoft Edge, etc.

You might wonder that if every web browser provides an interface to the user and allows them to connect with the web, then why are there so many web browsers? If we look at the history of web browsers, we can tell a lot about their special features and developing techniques. Before web browsers came into existence, computers were more like boxes that used command-line interfaces to perform some tasks. The development of web browsers revolutionized the entire way of interacting with a computer.

- ❖ In 1990, when Tim Berners-Lee, developed the first ever browser named "WorldWideWeb", at CERN (A European organization for nuclear research). It was indeed an extraordinary development as it was the only web browser present at that time which provided a user-friendly interface.

- ❖ In 1993, everyone started becoming familiar with the concept of web browsers and was curious to develop the same. This led to the invention of the "Mosaic" by NCSA (National Centre for Supercomputing Applications) at the University of Illinois. It gained massive popularity as it was the first graphical browser that demonstrated the use of multimedia (images) on the web.

- ❖ In 1994, another browser called "Netscape", founded by Andreessen turned out to be a success. It was the first web browser to be made public and gained immense popularity.

- ❖ In 1995, the world witnessed a race to develop better web browsers with attractive versions. It was this year when Microsoft developed the "Internet Explorer" and released it resulting in so-called "browser wars".

Picture 1.2: Tim Berners-Lee with first browser WorldWideWeb.

3. Addressing Web Pages

The World Wide Web comprises a series of large-capacity computers, known as "web servers", which are connected to the internet via telephone lines and satellites. The web servers each use the HyperText Transfer Protocol (HTTP) as a common communication standard to allow any computer connected to any web server to access files across the web. HTML web pages are merely plain text files that have been saved with a ".htm" or ".html" file extension, such as **index.html**.

- **Tips for you**
  A web page address (URL) cannot contain any blank space.
  Where an address states only the HTTP protocol and a domain name, most web servers are configured to seek a file named **index.html** in their default directory.

In order to access a web file, its web address must be entered into the address field of the web browser. The web address is formally known as its "Uniform Resource Locator" (URL) and typically has three parts:

- **Protocol** – any URL using the HTTP protocol begins by specifying the protocol as **http://** or secure **https://**
- **Domain** – the host name of the computer from which the file can be downloaded. For instance, **www.example.com**
- **Path** – the virtual path to the file on the named domain, including any parent directory names where applicable. For instance, **/hddocs/index.html**

A URL describing the location of a file by protocol, domain, and path is stating its "absolute address". So the absolute address of the file described by the protocol, domain, and path components above is **http://www.example.com/htdocs/index.html**

Code contained within an HTML web page can reference other HTML files in any domain by their absolute address. HTML files resident within the same domain can also be referenced more simply by their "relative address", which means that files located within the same directory can be referenced just by their file name. For instance, a file named "adjacent.html" located in the same directory can be referenced simply as **adjacent.html**.

Additionally, a relative address can reference a file within the parent directory by prefixing its name with "../". For instance, a file named "higher.html" in the parent directory can be referenced from the current directory as **../higher.html**.

4. How Do Web Servers Work?

When you enter a URL into the browser address field, the browser first examines the protocol. Where the protocol is specified as HTTP, or assumed to be HTTP if unspecified, the browser recognizes that a file is being sought from a web server. It then contacts a Domain Name Server (DNS) to look up the numerical Internet Protocol (IP) address of the specified domain name. Next, a connection is established with the web server at that IP address to request the file at the specified path. When the file is successfully located, it is copied back to the browser. Otherwise, the web server sends an error code, such as "404 – Page Not Found". The picture 1.3 shows how the web server works.

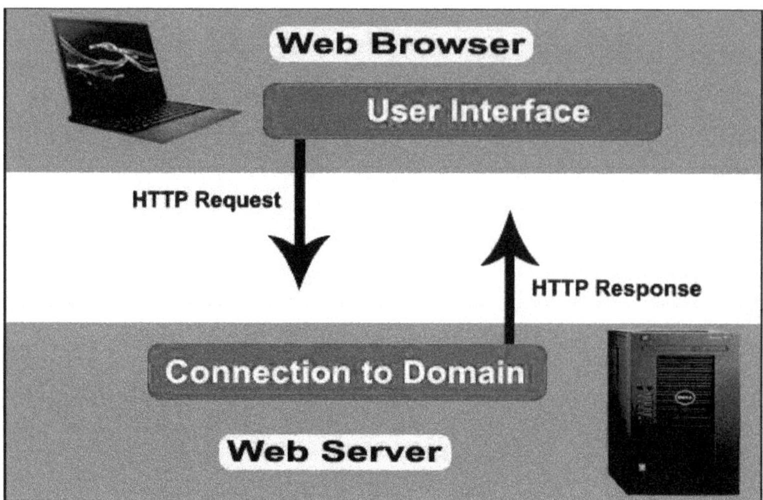

Picture 1.3: The function of web server.

- **Hot tips**
  The Domain Name Server is typically run by your Internet Service Provider or by your company.

A successful response sends HTTP headers to the web browser, describing the nature of the response, along with a copy of the requested file. You should know that the HTTP headers are not normally visible but can be examined using various development tools, such as the F12 Developer Tools feature in the Microsoft Edge web browser. Picture 1.4 indicating with an arrow shows the result when you press F12 on Microsoft Edge. Notice the headers in the picture 1.2 that he Content-Type is "text/html" – the MIME type used by all web servers to describe plain text HTML files.

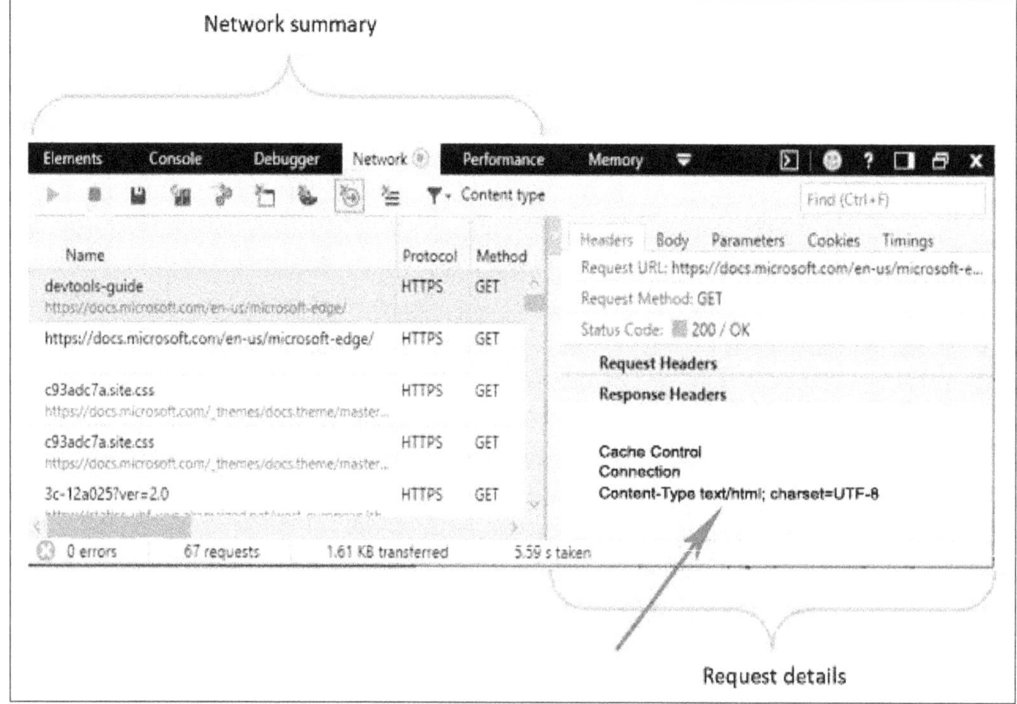

Picture 1.4: The HTTP headers.

5. Defining Document Structure

The structure of an HTML5 document has these three parts:

- **Document type Declaration** – declaring precisely which version of HTML is used to mark up the document
- **Head section** – providing descriptive data about the document itself, such as the document's title and the character set used
- **Body section** – containing the content that is to appear when the document gets loaded into a web browser

Document type declaration

The document type declaration must appear at the start of the first line of every HTML5 document to ensure the web browser will "render" (display) the document in "Standards Mode" – following the HTML5 specifications. The document type declaration tag for all HTML5 documents looks like this:

<!DOCTYPE HTML>

It is important to note that HTML5 is not a case-sensitive language – so the document type declaration tag, and all other tags, may alternatively be written in any combination of uppercase and lowercase characters. For example, the following are all valid:

<!DOCTYPE html>

<!Doctype Html>

<!doctype html>

The choice of capitalization is yours, but it is recommended you adhere consistently to whichever style you choose. The document type declaration tag capitalization style favored throughout this book uses all uppercase to emphasize its prominence as the very first tag on each page – but all other tags are in all lowercase. The document type declaration in earlier versions of HTML was part of the Standard Generalized Markup Language (SGML) from which HTML is derived.

Those familiar with previous versions of HTML may be surprised at the simplicity of the HTML5 document type declaration. In fact, the document type declaration in earlier versions was not actually part of the HTML language – so required lengthy references to schema documents. By contrast, the HTML5 document type declaration is an intrinsic part of HTML itself.

The entire document head section and body section can be enclosed within a pair of **<html> </html>** tags to contain the rest of the document. The HTML5 specification actually states that these are optional, but it is logical to provide a single "root" element. Most HTML tags are used in pairs like this to act as "containers" with the syntax **<tagname>** data **</tagname>.** An HTML "element" is any matching pair of opening and closing tags, or any single tag not requiring a closing tag – as described in the HTML5 element tags at the end of this book.

Head section

The head's section begins with an HTML opening **<head>** tag and ends with a corresponding closing **</head>** tag. Data describing the document can be added later between these two tags to complete the HTML document's head section.

Body section

The document's body section begins with an HTML opening **<body>** tag and ends with a corresponding closing **</body>** tag. Data content to appear in the browser can be added later between these two tags to complete the HTML document's body section.

Code comments

There is the place of comments within the head and body section. You can add comments at any point within both the head and body section between a pair of **<!- -** and **- ->** tags. Anything that appears between the comment tags is ignored by the browser. The "invisible" characters that represent tabs, newlines, carriage returns, and spaces are collectively known as "whitespace". They may optionally be used to inset the tags for clarity in your HTML5 document.

Fundamental structure

Here is the fundamental structure of the first document. You need to understand each markup tags as described in the previous sections. The markup tags that create the fundamental structure of every HTML5 document look like this:

```
<!DOCTYPE HTML>

<html>
   <head>
      <!-- Data describing the document to be added here -->
   </head>

   <body>
      <!-- Data content to appear in the browser to be added here -->
   </body>

</html>
```

Picture 1.5: The HTML fundamental structure.

On the next page, we will create an HTML document. The fundamental HTML5 document structure, described above in the Fundamental Structure section, can be used to create a simple HTML5 document in any plain text editor – such as Windows' Notepad application.

Project 1 – My First Heading

Here is the first HTML document we are going to create. The fundamental HTML5 document can be created in any plain text editor, such as Windows Notepad application.

1. Type this code in your Notepad without copy-paste as you need to learn the coding.

```
<!DOCTYPE html>
<html>
<head>
<title>Page Title</title>
</head>
<body>

<h1>My First Heading</h1>
<p>My first paragraph.</p>

</body>
</html>
```

2. Once you type the code, save this document with the name "Project1.html" while setting **Encoding** to the popular "UTF-8" format.

3. Open this "**Project1.html**" document in a web browser. For that, you need to right click on the document icon and select **Google Chrome** to open.

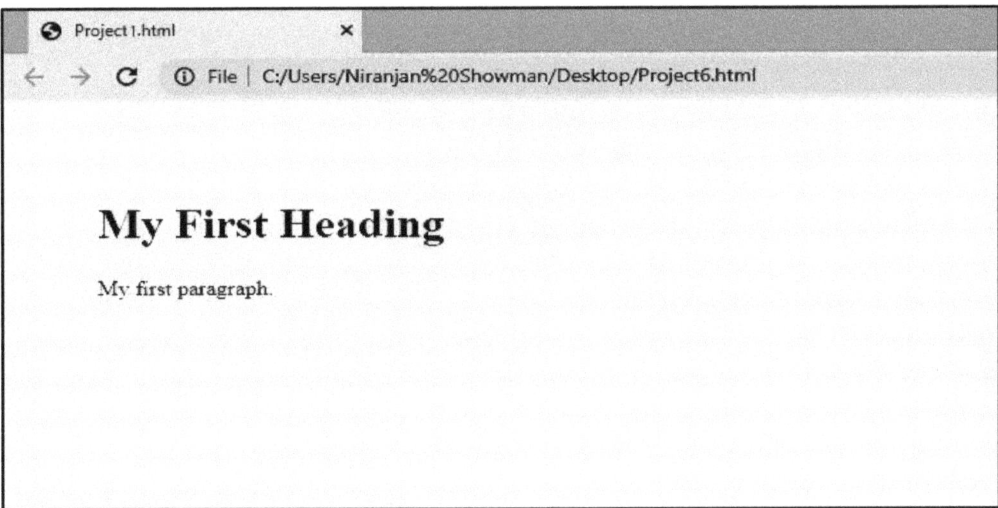

Picture 1.6: The first HTML document.

This is called the valid "barebones" HTML5 document where the information must first be added defining the document's primary language, its character encoding format, and its title. The purpose of a web browser (Chrome, Edge, Firefox, Safari) is to read HTML documents and display them correctly. A browser does not display the HTML tags, but uses them to determine how to display the document.

Example Explained: -

- The **<!DOCTYPE html>** declaration defines that this document is an HTML5 document.
- The **<html>** element is the root element of an HTML page.
- The **<head>** element contains meta information about the HTML page.
- The **<title>** element specifies a title for the HTML page (which is shown in the browser's title bar or in the page's tab).
- The **<body>** element defines the document's body, and is a container for all the visible contents, such as headings, paragraphs, images, hyperlinks, tables, lists, etc.
- The **<h1>** element defines a large heading.
- The **<p>** element defines a paragraph.

Start tag	Element content	End tag
<h1>	My First Heading	</h1>
<p>	My first paragraph.	</p>

What is an HTML Element?

An HTML element is defined by a start tag, some content, and an end tag, and below is a visualization of an HTML page structure. The content inside the <body> section will be displayed in a browser. The content inside the <title> element will be shown in the browser's title bar or in the page's tab.

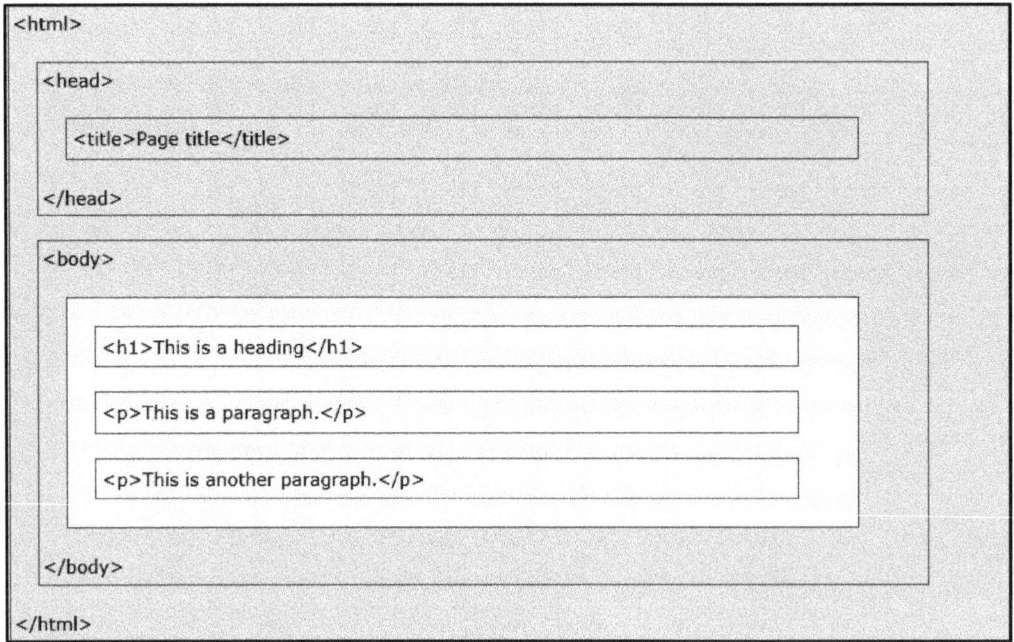

Picture 1.7: The visualization of HTML page structure.

6. HTML History

HTML language that has its own syntax and rules, must be followed for any purposeful website creation. Imagine you want to make a digital invite for Christmas with the occasion, date, and venue. You want the occasion to be in a bigger font and the date and venue in a smaller font. Now, you can use HTML to write a set of instructions or rules to tell your computer how to display the invite. Since the early days of the World Wide Web, there have been many versions of HTML.

Year	Version
1989	Tim Berners-Lee invented www
1991	Tim Berners-Lee invented HTML
1993	Dave Raggett drafted HTML+
1995	HTML Working Group defined HTML 2.0
1997	W3C Recommendation: HTML 3.2
1999	W3C Recommendation: HTML 4.01
2000	W3C Recommendation: XHTML 1.0
2008	WHATWG HTML5 First Public Draft
2012	WHATWG HTML5 Living Standard
2014	W3C Recommendation: HTML5
2016	W3C Candidate Recommendation: HTML 5.1
2017	W3C Recommendation: HTML5.1 2nd Edition
2017	W3C Recommendation: HTML5.2

Picture 1.8: The versions of HTML.

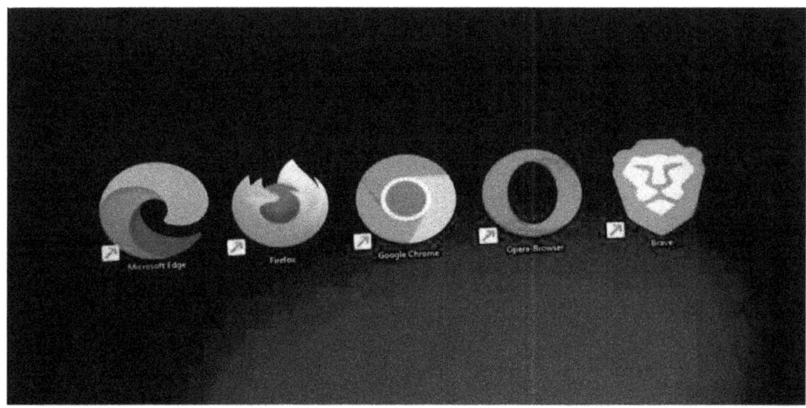

7. Validating Documents

Just as text documents may contain spelling and grammar errors, HTML documents may contain various errors that prevent them from conforming to the specification rules. In order to verify that HTML document does indeed conform to the rules of its specified document type declaration, it can be tested by a validator tool. Only HTML documents that pass the validation test successfully are sure to be valid documents.

Web browsers make not attempt at validation, so it is well worth verifying every HTML document with a validator tool before it is published, even when the content looks fine in your web browser. When the browser encounters HTML errors it will make a guess at what is intended – but different browsers can make different interpretations so may display the document incorrectly. Conversely, valid HTML documents should always appear correctly in any standards-compliant browser. The World Wide Web Consortium (W3C) provides a free online validator tool that checks the syntax of web documents:

1. With an internet connection, open your web browser and navigate to the W3C Validator Tool at **validator.w3.org**.

2. When this web page is open, click on the "Validate by File Upload" tab and upload your **"Project1.html"** document by clicking **Choose File** button.

3. Finally click the **Check** button to examine if your document has any error.

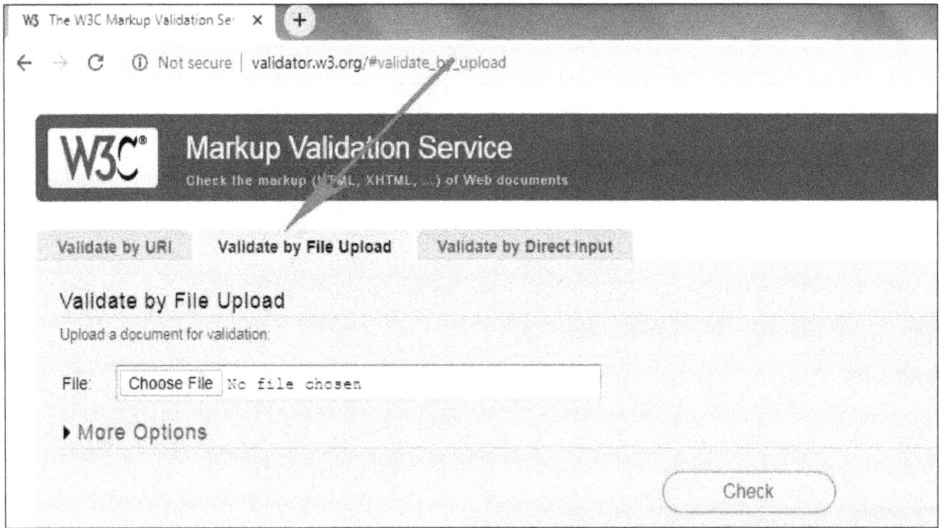

Picture 1.9: The W3C validator.

- **Hot tips**

   Other tabs in the validator allow you to enter the web address of an HTML document located on a web server to "Validate by URI" or copy and paste all code from a document to "Validate by Direct Input". URI stands for Uniform Resource Identifier.

   The validator's "Check" button is to upload an HTML document that runs the validation test – the results will then be displayed.

Chapter 2

HTML Editor, Page Information, Attributes

An HTML Editor is a software application designed to help users create and modify HTML code. It often includes features like syntax highlighting, tag completion, and error detection, which facilitate the coding process. There are two main types of HTML editors:

- **Text-Based Editors** – Allow direct coding with features like syntax highlighting and code completion for full control over the webpage structure. Example – Sublime Text, Visual Studio Code, etc.

- **WYSIWYG (What You See Is What You Get) Editors** – Offer a graphical interface to design web pages visually, automatically generating the corresponding HTML code. Example – Adobe Dreamweaver, etc.

1. Employing HTML Editor

HTML code can be created in any plain text editor that provides encoding in the recommended UTF-8 format. As long as the code in the new text file is saved with a file extension of ".html" or ".htm", an HTML5 document is created. This file can then be opened in any web browser, such as Microsoft Edge, to see how the HTML code is interpreted to "render" (display) the content on the screen. Older web browsers, such as Internet Explorer 8 or earlier, will not fully recognize the modern HTML5 markup code. It is best, therefore, to view HTML5 web pages in the latest version of the Microsoft Edge, Internet Explorer, Firefox, Google Chrome, Opera, and Safari web browsers.

Some HTML authors prefer to use specialized HTML editors that colorize the various parts of the source code for greater clarity, and offer further features. Microsoft Expression web editor, shown in the picture below, is a popular choice for some HTML authors. Expression Web 4 is available free for download at **microsoft.com/en-us/download/details.aspx?id=36179**.

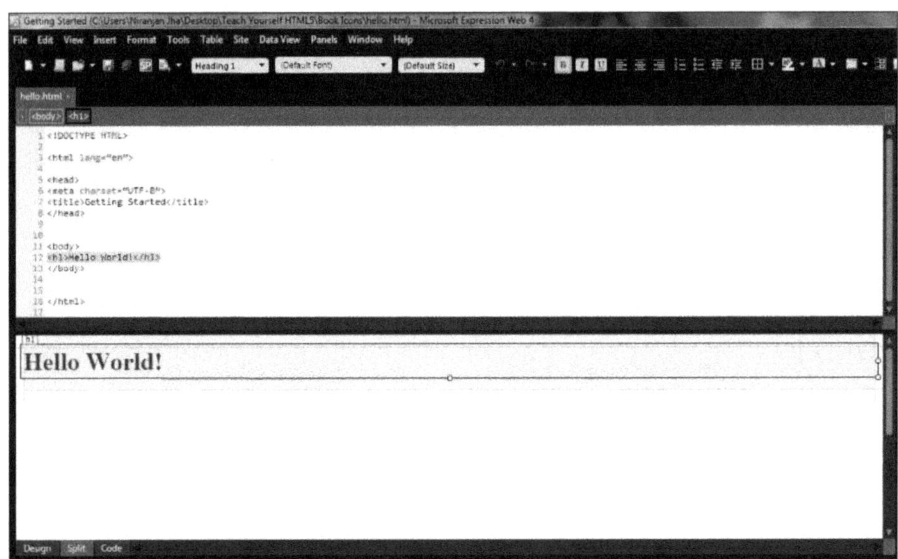

Picture 2.1: Microsoft Expression web editor.

The Split view at the bottom left side in Expression Web provides a live preview of what the HTML document will look like in a web browser, as shown in the picture 2.1. Additionally, when you go ahead and click File> Preview in Browser, a built-in menu lets you quickly view the document in any web browser installed on your computer.

- **Hot tips**
  The Expression Web interface also allows web pages to be created visually by dragging components onto its Design window – but knowledge of HTML is often helpful in fine-tuning the web page.
  The W3C online validator tool can also be used to verify correct HTML code, along with Expression Web's Compatibility Checker tool.
  Expression Web also provides a customizable Code Snippet facility to quickly insert frequently used chunks of code – press **Ctrl + Enter** to see the Code Snippet list.

Expression Web's "Compatibility Checker" tool lets you easily locate code errors that do not conform to the declared document type. Additionally, like other Microsoft development tools, the Expression Web editor has "IntelliSense", which identifies syntax errors live as you type the HTML code. This feature also provides context-sensitive menus that can insert HTML tags compatible with the current point in the document. For example, when you type "<" in the head section, IntelliSense presents a list of tags that may be inserted at that point. After selecting a tag and typing a space, IntelliSense then present a list of attributes that may be inserted within that tag.

By default, IntelliSense automatically inserts a matching closing tag, if appropriate, whenever you type an opening tag. Some authors dislike this ability, but the Expression Web options allow IntelliSense features to be turned on and off individually to customize the editor to your personal taste.

2. Providing Page Information

This section demonstrates how the head section of an HTML5 document can describe the document, incorporate scripts for functionality, and add style sheets for presentation. In this chapter, you will learn: Bestowing a title, Specifying a character set, Refreshing the page, Describing the document, Incorporating scripts, Incorporating style sheets, and Linking more resources.

Bestowing a title

The specification requires every HTML5 document to have a title, but its importance is often overlooked. The document title should be carefully considered, however, as it is used extensively:

- **Bookmarks** – save the document title to link back to its URL
- **Title Bar** – a web browser window may display the title
- **Navigation Tab** – a web browser tab may display the title
- **History** – saves the document title to link back to its URL
- **Search Engines** – read the document title and typically display it in search results to link back to its URL

Document title should ideally be short and meaningful – each tab on a modern tabbed browser may display only 10 characters. After mentioning these specification, I mention some hot tips to help you understand things more clearly.

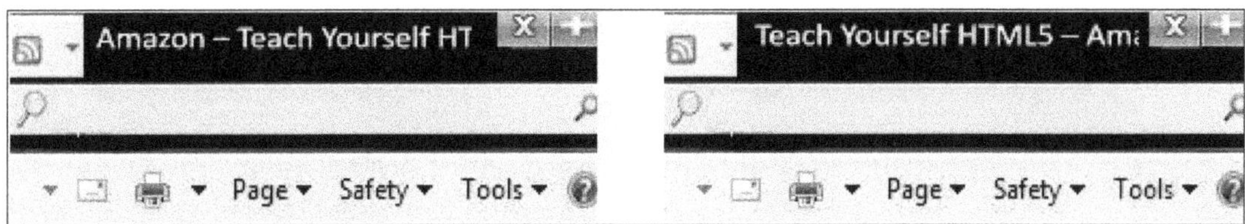

Picture 2.2: The HTML5 document having a title.

Document titles throughout a website should follow a consistent naming convention and capitalize all major words. One popular naming convention provides a personal or company name and brief page description separated by a hyphen. For example, "Amazon – Teach Yourself HTML5". An alternative places the description first, so it remains visible when the title is truncated. For example, "Teach Yourself HTML5 – Amazon". For illustration purpose, the title naming is shown in the next picture 2.2.

Document titles, and document content, may contain special characters that are known in HTML5 as "entities". Each entity reference begins with an ampersand and ends with a semi-colon. For example, the entity, **<** (less than) creates a "<" character and the entity **>** (greater than) creates a ">" character. These are often needed to avoid confusion with the angled brackets that surround each HTML tag. Other frequently used entities include ** ** (a single non-breaking space), **©** ©, **®** (®), and **™** (™). These are best avoided in document titles, however, as the vocal narrator used by visually impaired viewers may read each entity character as a word.

Project 2 – Adding Title
In this project, you are going to learn about inserting an entity within the title element in an HTML5 document. Now write this code in your Notepad and save as Project2.html.

```
<!DOCTYPE html>
<html>

<head>
<meta charset="UTF-8">
<title>
&lt;Teach Yourself HTML5&gt;
</title>

</head>

<body>
<h1>Project Two</h1>
</body>

</html>
```

Example Explained: -

- The **<meta charset="UTF-8">** element sets UTF-8 character for a webpage.
- The **<Teach Yourself HTML5>** element inserts a title including entities.
- The **<h1>** element defines a large heading.

When you save this document with the name project2.html, setting **Encoding** to the popular "UTF-8" format, your web browser will show the document with title as <Teach Yourself HTML5> shown in the picture below. If you wish, you can change the syntax: ~~<Teach Yourself HTML5>~~ to **quot;Teach Yourself HTML5"** and this will result in title as title as "Teach Yourself HTML5".

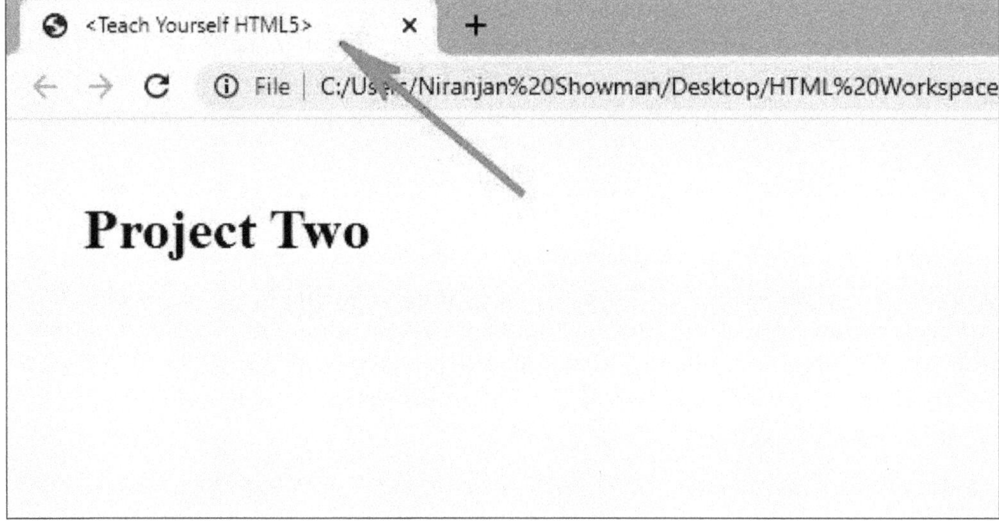

Picture 2.3: The webpage showing title.

- **Hot tips**
  The quotation marks: "..." are very important while creating an HTML document in Notepad. Always, make sure you type the correct quotation mark and also check that it appears correctly and not in the reverse order. Never copy-paste the syntax but always type it entirely.

Project 3 – HTML Headings

HTML headings are defined with the <h1> to <h6> tags. The <h1> defines the most important heading while <h6> defines the least important heading.

```
<!DOCTYPE html>
<html>
<body>

<h1>This is heading 1</h1>
<h2>This is heading 2</h2>
<h3>This is heading 3</h3>
<h4>This is heading 4</h4>
<h5>This is heading 5</h5>
<h6>This is heading 6</h6>

</body>
</html>
```

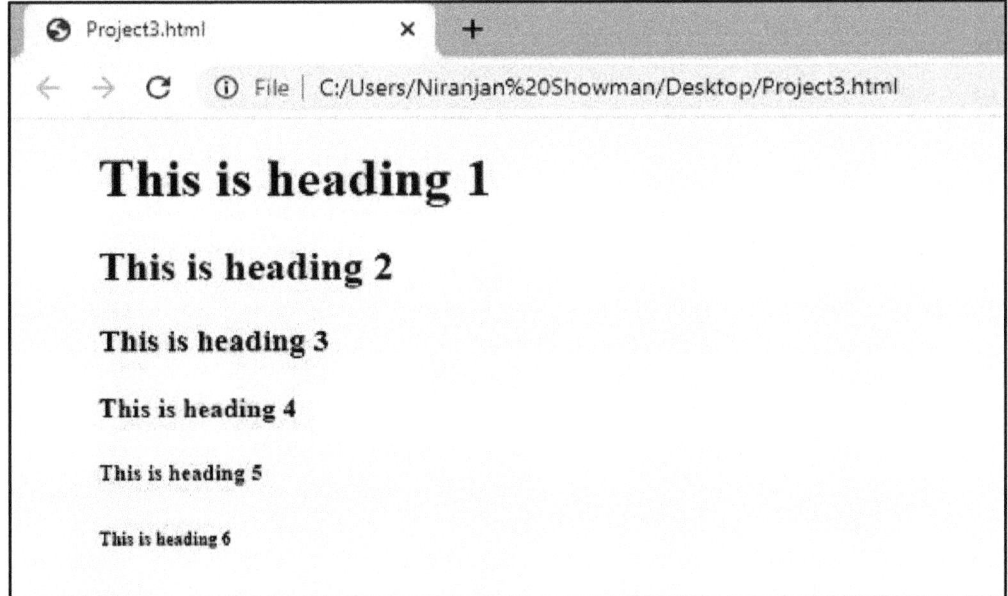

Picture 2.4: The result of different headings.

Specifying a character set

The examples in this book are all saved with Unicode files endings using the UTF-8 character-set. This character-set supports all characters in both Western and English languages, which allows the HTML document to contain characters from any language. Further character sets that exist also support all languages, while others exclusively support Western languages. The five most popular character-sets are listed below:

Name:	Character Set:
UTF-8	Multi-lingual Universal Transformation Format
BIG5	Multi-lingual traditional Chinese characters
SHIFT_JIS	Multi-lingual traditional Japanese characters
US-ASCII	US ASCII standard Western alphabet characters
ISO-8859-1	ISO standard Western alphabet characters

Character-set names are not case-sensitive – so "BIG5", "Big5", and "big5" are equivalent. To create a web page in English, you need to use only UTF-8 character-set. US ASCII was formerly the most commonly used encoding on the web, but it has now been surpassed by UTF-8 due to its wider support. If you want to insert a different language, you need the text editor of that particular language. After knowing about the different character-sets, you would get acquainted to Meta information in the next section.

3. HTML Attributes

HTML Attributes are special words used within the opening tag of an HTML element. They provide additional information about HTML elements. HTML attributes are used to configure and adjust the element's behavior, appearance, or functionality in a variety of ways. Each attribute has a name and a value, formatted as **name="value".** Attributes tell the browser how to render the element or how it should behave during user interactions.

Refreshing the page

Meta information is simply the data that describes other data. In the context of HTML, document meta data describes the document itself – rather than the document's contents. HTML meta data is defined in the head section of the HTML document using the **<meta>** tag. Previous examples have used this tag to specify the document's character-set – as one piece of information describing that document. Further **<meta>** tags can be added to describe other aspects of the document.

The **<meta>** tag is an "empty" tag that needs no matching closing tag to create an HTML document in your Notepad. It is only used to specify information with its tag attributes. For example, its **http-equiv** attribute can represent a document HTTP header property and its **content** attribute specify that property's value. Assigning the HTTP "refresh" property to a **<meta>** tag's **http-equiv** attribute can be used to reload the page after a number of seconds specified by its **content** attribute. For example, to reload the page after five seconds, like this:

<meta http-equiv="refresh" content= "5">

This technique is often used on websites to dynamically update news or status items, as it does not depend on JavaScript support. Another popular use redirects the browser to a new web page after a specified number of seconds, as mentioned below. Make sure you type (not copy-paste) the correct quotation mark and also check that it appears correctly and not in the reverse order.

<meta http-equiv="refresh" content= "5 ; url='new-page.html' ">

Project 4 – HTML Attribute

In this project, the **<meta>** tag's **content** attribute specifies both the number of seconds to delay and the new URL to load. The result will come as your browser getting redirected to another page. Follow the steps carefully and type the syntax with correct quote marks.

1. Create a folder (directory) on your desktop with the name **Cromosys**.

2. Start with the HTML5 document type declaration by typing the following code:

```
<!DOCTYPE HTML>
<head>

<title>Refresh Example</title>
</head>
<meta charset="UTF-8">

<meta http-equiv="refresh" content="5 ; url='new-page.html' ">

<body>
<h1>Moving in 5 Seconds...</h1>
</body>
</html>
```

3. Save this document with the name: **refesh.html** in the Cromosys folder, and close your Notepad application. You don't need to open it in a browser at this moment.

Example Explained: -

- The **<meta charset="UTF-8">** element sets UTF-8 character for a webpage.
- The **<meta http-equiv="refresh" content="5 ; url='new-page.html' ">** HTML meta http-equiv attribute defines a time interval for the document to refresh itself.

4. Now, you will create another document to which the browser will redirect.

```
<!DOCTYPE HTML>
<head>

<meta charset="UTF-8">
<title>Refresh Example - New</title>
</head>

<body>
<h1>Moved Here After 5 Seconds!</h1>
</body>
</html>
```

5. You need to save this second document also in the same folder (directory) **Cromosys** with the file name as: **new-page.html.**

6. Open the first document **refresh.html** in your favorite browser and wait up to 5 seconds. You will see the browser gets redirected after a five second delay to your second web page. Both instances are shown in the picture below.

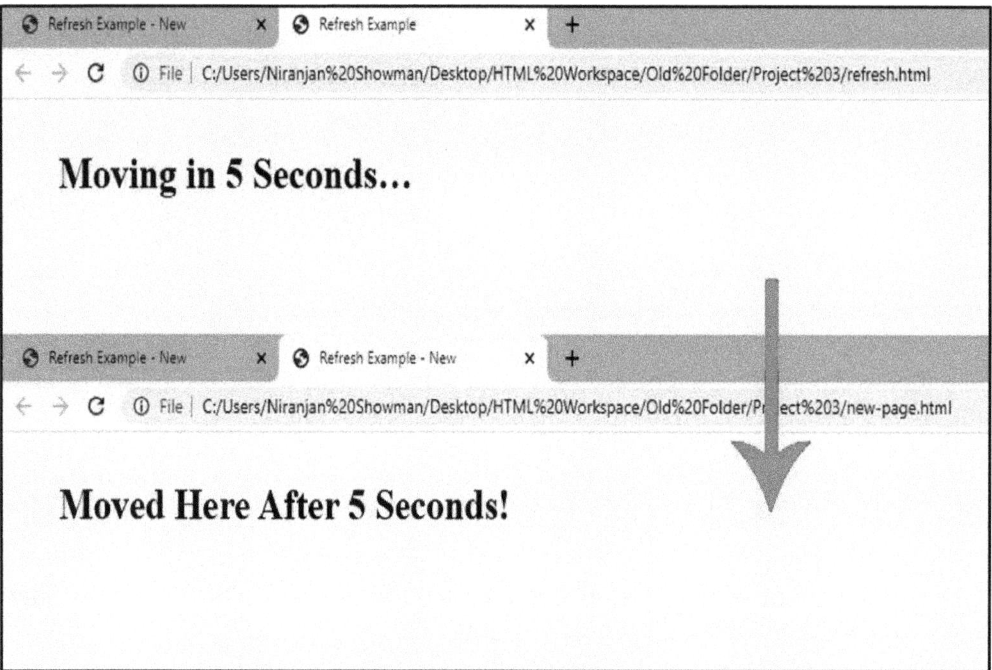

Picture 2.5: The result of HTML page refreshing attribute.

The result comes only when the entire syntax is typed properly with correct quote marks, and not copy-paste. Also, make sure you save both of the files into the same folder or directory. Notice that the content attribute value entirely surrounds both the delay and URL with double quote marks, but the URL is just surrounded by single quote marks.

Describing the document
In addition to specifying the document's character-set and expiry date, **<meta>** tags can be used to provide descriptive information that may be useful to search engines. This offers no guarantee of high ranking, however, as search engines also use other page information for that purpose – especially the document title. Nevertheless, it is helpful to provide a description and a list of keywords relevant to the contents of that page so that search engine "spiders" might usefully add the page to their index.

- **Hot tips**
  All search engine spiders find pages to add to their index – even if the page has never been submitted to them.
  Always include the three most important keywords in the description.

Descriptive **<meta>** tags always have a **name** attribute, but to specify a page feature, and a **content** attribute to specify that feature's value. For example, the "description" name allows you to specify text content describing the page. This should be short, succinct sentences that might appear in a search engine's results page. Any description longer than around 200 characters may get truncated.

Similarly, you need to understand that the "keywords" name allows you to specify text content in the format of a comma-separated list of relevant keywords. These may be used by search engines to influence their results. For example, a search for "italian ceramics" could return all web pages with "italian" and "ceramics" in their keywords list. Promotion of the web page by keywords in best achieved by following some simple guidelines:

- Use only lowercase characters
- Keep all keywords on a single line
- Never repeat a keyword in a list
- Limit the keywords list to 1,000 characters or less
- Try to use the plural form for keywords – to match searches made with both the singular and plural forms of that word

Project 5 – Using Keywords For Webpage

HTML allows you to specity keywords for your webpage that help search engines to index it. The "computer bots" read the keywords of webpages and show them accordingly. Here is the code that teaches you to insert keywords for a webpage.

```
<!DOCTYPE HTML>
<head>
<meta charset="UTF-8">

<meta name="description"
content="Shop for beautiful Italian Ceramics, Tuscan Majolica, Home Décor, and more.">

<meta name="keywords"
content="Tuscan,Italian,ceramics,home décor,majolica,dinnerwares,vases,plates,bowls">

  <title> Tuscan Home Decor [Italian Ceramics] </title>
</head>
<body> <h1> Beautiful Tuscan Ceramics </h1> </body>
</html>
```

1. Save this file with the name: project5.html in Notepad setting Encoding always as UTF-8.

2. To see the page info and keywords of this webpage, right-click somewhere on Chrome page and click **View Page Source**.

3. To have a better view, open this html document in Firefox browser, and select **View Page Info**. The Page Info shows description and keywords which is the meta data of your page.

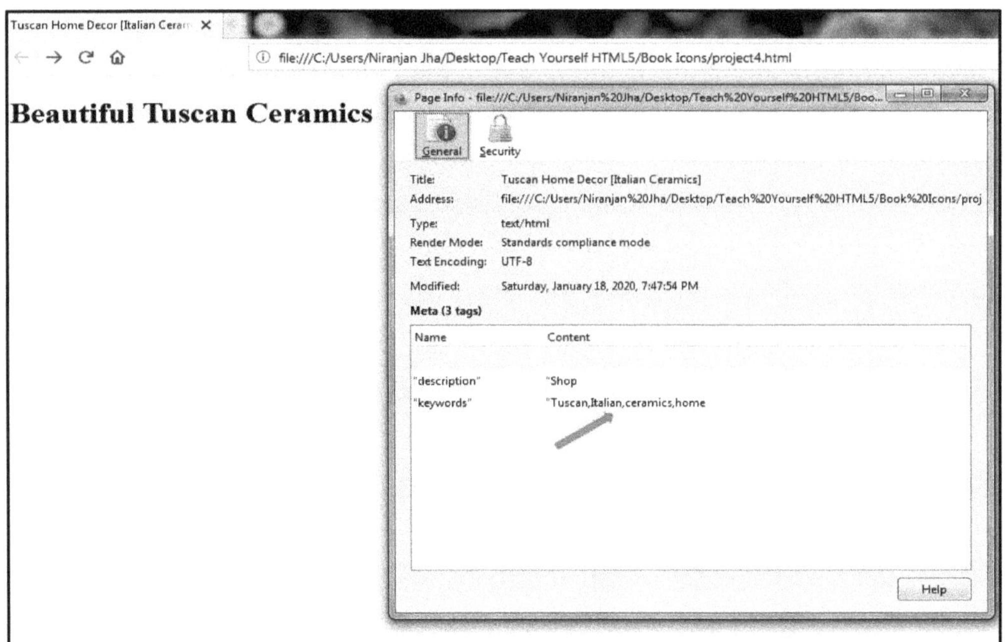

Picture 2.6: Firefox showing webpage info and keywords.

Example Explained: -

- The code **<meta name="description"** is meta element to specify the description.
- The code **<meta name="keywords"** is meta element to specify keywords.

You can notice that the first four meta keywords in this example also appears in the meta description. There are a number of free meta tag generators available online – enter "free meta tag generator" into a search engine.

4. HTML Superior Attributes

We will discuss about some more HTML attributes that provide additional information about HTML elements. As we already know that:

- All HTML elements can have **attributes**
- Attributes provide **additional information** about elements
- Attributes are always specified in the **start tag**
- Attributes usually come in name/value pairs like: **name="value"**

Project 6 – The href Attribute

The **href** attribute in HTML specifies the URL of a link. It's used within the <a> tag, which is also known as the anchor element. The href attribute is the acronym of Hypertext REFerence.

```
<!DOCTYPE html>
<html>
<body>

<h2>The href Attribute</h2>

<p>HTML links are defined with the a tag. The link address is specified in the href attribute:</p>

<a href="https://www.facebook.com/cromosys">Visit Cromosys</a>

</body>
</html>
```

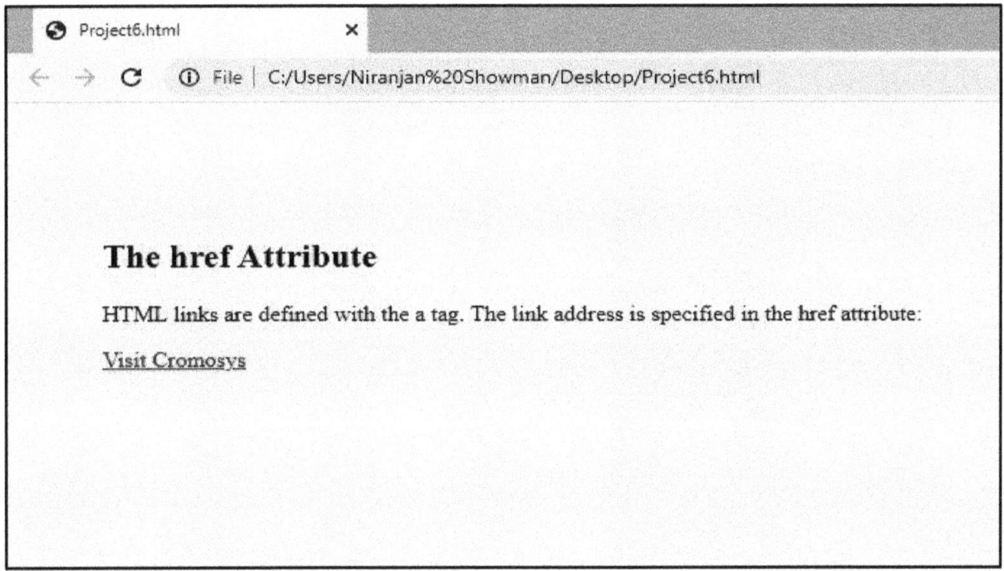

Picture 2.7: The result of href attribute.

Project 7 – The src Attribute

The <img> tag is used to embed an image in an HTML page. The **src** attribute specifies the path to the image to be displayed. The Img attribute src stands for "source" of your Image location.

```
<!DOCTYPE html>
<html>
<body>

<h2>The src Attribute</h2>
<p>HTML images are defined with the img tag, and the filename of the image source is specified in the src attribute:</p>

<img src="football.jpg" width="500" height="600">
</body>
</html>
```

1. Place an **image file** on your desktop. In my case I have put football.jpg.

2. Write the above mentioned code in Notepad and save it as Project7.html also on **desktop**.

3. In **img src** element, write your image file name with **.jpg** extension. JPG and JPEG are the same file format, HTML understands .jpg.

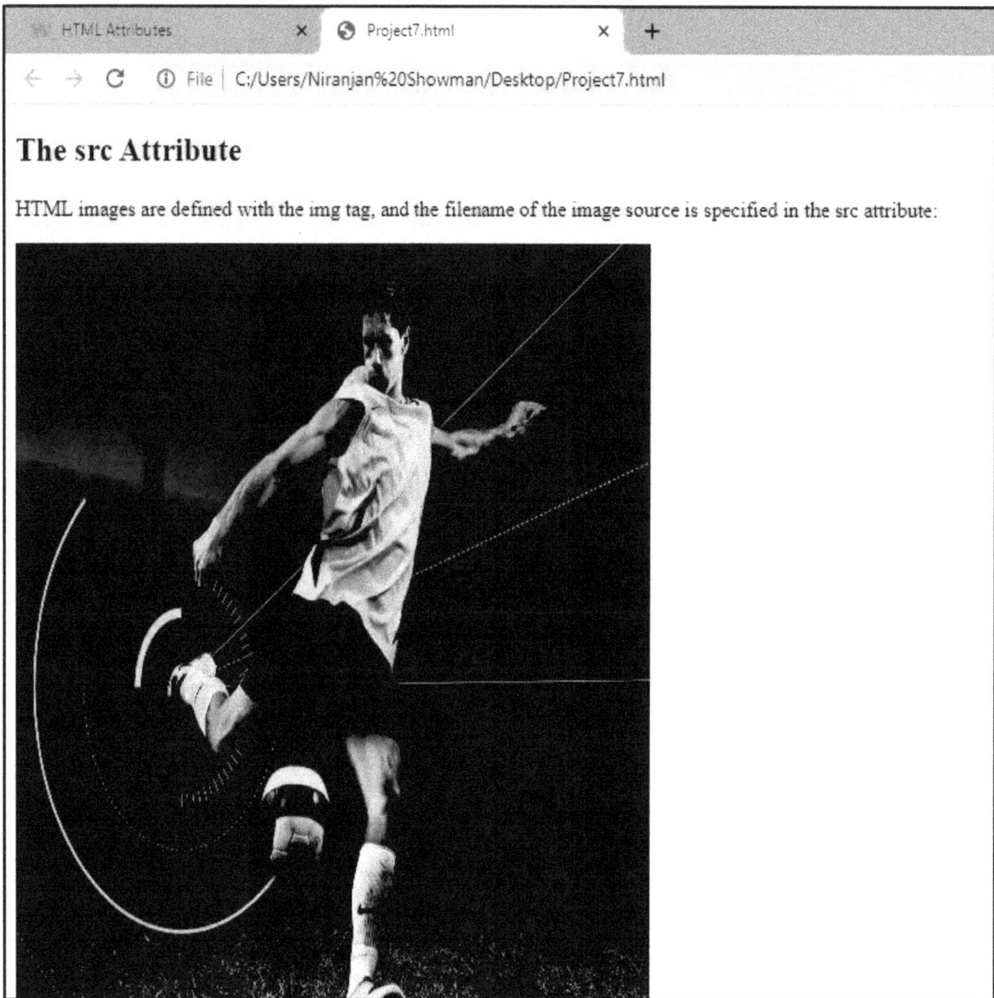

Picture 2.8: The result of scr attribute.

Things to undertand:-
There are two ways to specify the URL in the src attribute:

1. **Absolute URL** - Links to an external image that is hosted on another website. Example: src="https://www.facebook.com/cromosys/images/football.jpg".

Notes: External images might be under copyright. If you do not get permission to use it, you may be in violation of copyright laws. In addition, you cannot control external images; it can suddenly be removed or changed.

2. **Relative URL** - Links to an image that is hosted within the website. Here, the URL does not include the domain name. If the URL begins without a slash, it will be relative to the current page. Example: src="football.jpg". If the URL begins with a slash, it will be relative to the domain. Example: src="/images/football.jpg". It is always advisable to use relative URLs because they will not break if you change domain.

Project 8 – The style Attribute

The HTML style attribute is the rule that describe how a document will be presented in a browser. The style attribute is used to add styles to an element, such as color, font, size, and more. Here is the HTML code to use style attribute.

```html
<!DOCTYPE html>
<html>
<body>

<h2>The style Attribute</h2>
<p>The style attribute is used to add styles to an element, such as color:</p>

<p style="color:red;">This is a red paragraph.</p>
<p style="color:blue;">This is a blue paragraph.</p>

</body>
</html>
```

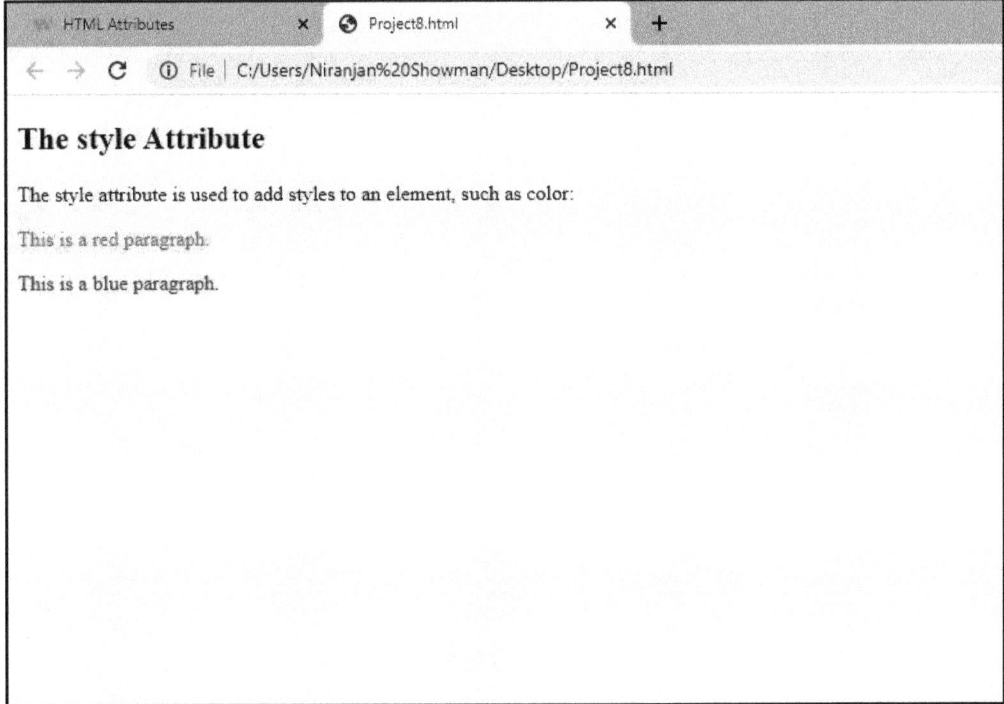

Picture 2.9: The result of style attribute.

Project 9 – The title Attribute

The title attribute defines some extra information about an element. The value of the title attribute will be displayed as a tooltip when you mouse over the element.

```
<!DOCTYPE html>
<html>
<body>

<h2 title="I'm a header">The title Attribute</h2>

<p title="I'm a tooltip">Mouse over this paragraph, to display the title attribute as a tooltip.</p>

</body>
</html>
```

Picture 2.10: The result of title attribute.

Things to undertand:-

When you move the mouse over "The title Attribute", it will display the title as "**I'm a header**". Similarly, when you move the mouse over the paragraph, it will display "**I'm a tooltip**".

- **Hot tips**
  We always suggest to use lowercase attributes. The HTML standard does not require uppercase attribute names. The title attribute (and all other attributes) can be written with uppercase or lowercase like **title** or **TITLE**.

We always suggest to quote attribute values. The HTML standard does not require quotes around attribute values. But we recommends quotes in HTML and demand quotes for all other documents.

If you ask, single or double quotes? Double quotes around attribute values are the most common in HTML, but single quotes can also be used. In some situations, when the attribute value itself contains double quotes, it is necessary to use single quotes.

5. Incorporating Style Sheets

Cascading Style Sheets file known as **CSS** file can be incorporated within HTML documents to describe the presentational aspects of each element on the page. The use of style sheets has replaced all features of HTML that formerly related to presentation. For example, the <font> tag has become obsolete, as font family, weight, style, and size are now specified by a style sheet rule.

Style sheets enclosed by **<style> </style>** tags can be added within the head section of an HTML document to enclose rules governing how the content will appear. The **<style>** tag automatically assumes a **type** attribute value of **"text/css"**, as style sheets are expected to use the Cascading Style Sheet language by default. This means that the **type** attribute can be omitted from the tag unless you are incorporating a style sheet that uses a different styling language. For example, a simple style sheet containing rules to determine the appearance of all size-one headings could look like this:

```
<style>
h1 { color : red ; background : yellow ; }
</style>
```

This is acceptable and will validate but, in line with the aim of HTML5 to separate content from presentation, style sheets are best contained within a separate file. The great advantage of placing style sheets and scripts in separate file is that they can be applied to multiple HTML documents – thus making website maintenance much easier. Editing a shared style sheet or script instantly affects such HTML document that shares that file. The <link > tag is a single tag and it does not have a matching closing tag. You can see the element tags list at the end of this book.

An external style sheet is incorporated within an HTML document by adding a **<link>** tag in the document's head section. This must contain a **rel** (relationship) attribute assigned a **"stylesheet"** value, and the URL of the style sheet must be assigned to its **href** attribute. Once again, this tag automatically assumes a **type** attribute value of **"text/css"** for style sheets, so the **type** attribute can be omitted unless you are incorporating a style sheet that uses a different styling language. For example, add an adjacent style sheet file named **"style.css"**, like this:

```
<link rel="stylesheet" href="style.css">
```

Project 10 – Incorporating Style Sheets

Cascading Style Sheets (CSS) is a stylesheet language used to describe the presentation of a document written in HTML. CSS is used to define styles for your web pages, including the design, layout and variations. You are going to create a CSS file named "style.css" in the same way as you created HTML5 document. For this, you need to create a folder with the name **Project 10** on your desktop.

```
<!DOCTYPE HTML>
<head>

<link rel="stylesheet" href="style.css">
<meta charset="UTF-8">
<title> Style Sheet Example </title>
</head>

<body>
<h1> Styled Heading </h1>
</body>
</html>
```

1. Write this code in Notepad without copy-paste to avoid any blank space. Blank spaces hinder the HTML code from functioning.

2. After writing this code precisely, save the file with the name "style.html" in **Project 10** folder. Make sure you type the file name in **lowercase** as mentioned, and set Encoding always as UTF-8.

3. Open **another** Notepad window and write the CSS code to incorporate with HTML document as mentioned below.

```
h1
{

        color : red ;
        background : yellow ;
        border : 10px dashed blue ;
        padding : 5px ;
        width : 550px ;


}
```

4. Save this Cascading Style Sheets (CSS) file with the name "style.css" in the same **Project 10** folder. Make sure you type the file name in **lowercase** as mentioned, and set Encoding always as UTF-8.

5. Now open the **style.html** file in your web browser to see the style rules applied. The picture is shown on the next page.

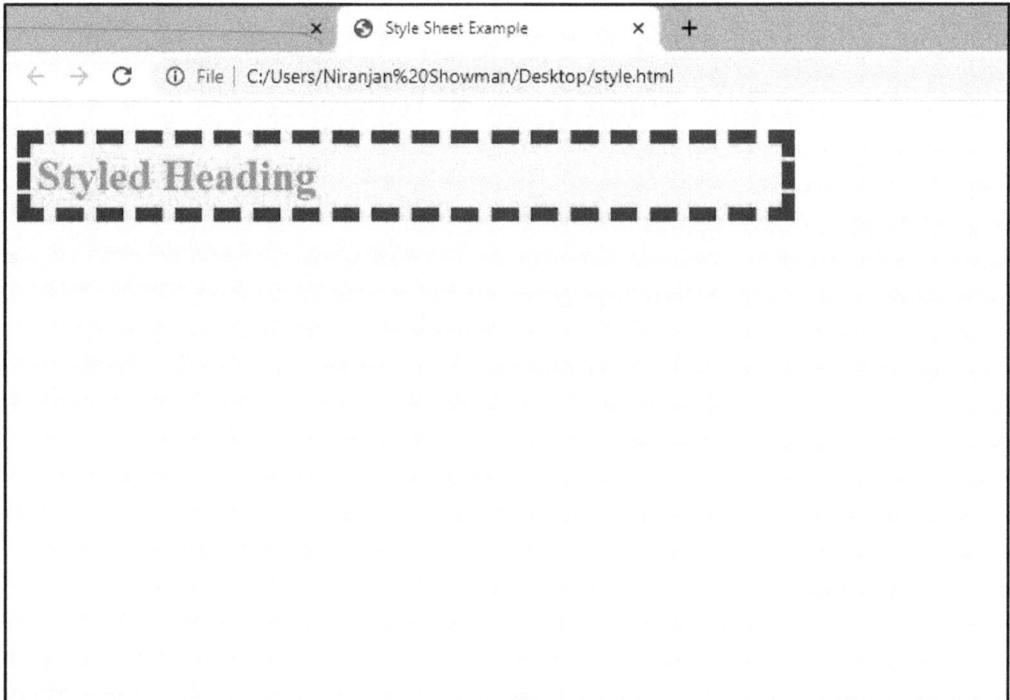

Picture 2.11: The result of incorporating style sheets.

6. Incorporating Scripts

Scripts can be incorporated within HTML documents to interact with the user and to provide dynamic effects. This ability has become increasingly important with the development of Web 2.0 pages in which sections of the page can be dynamically updated. Previously, the browser would typically request an entire new page from the web server, which was less efficient and more cumbersome, so Web 2.0 is a great improvement.

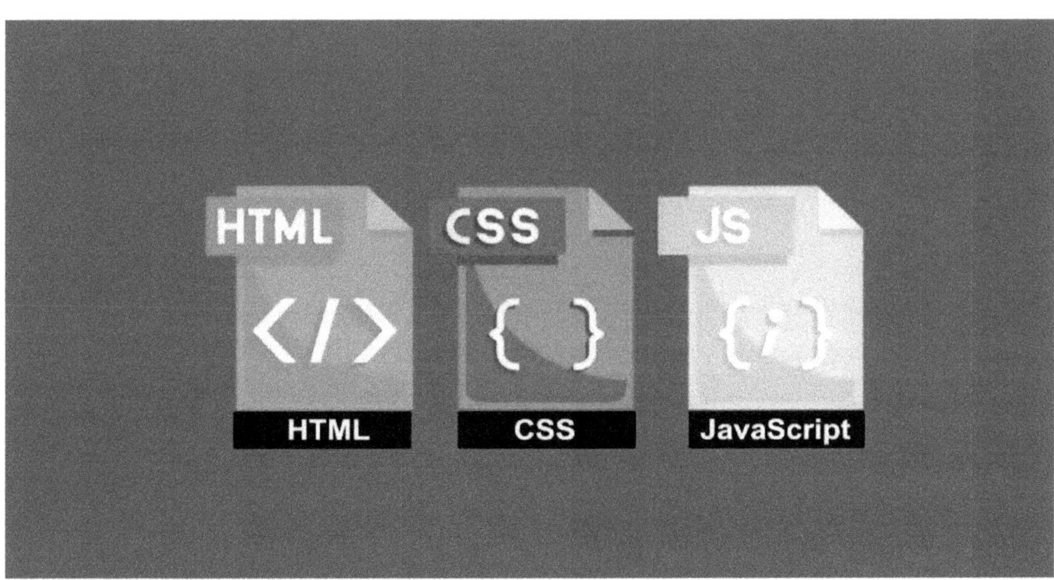

Scripts enclosed by **<script> </script>** tags can be added within the head section of an HTML document but, in line with the aim of HTML5 to separate content from presentation, are best contained in a separate file. The **<script>** tag automatically assumes a **type** attribute value of **"text/javascript"**, as scripts are expected to use the JavaScript language by default. This means that the **type** attribute can be omitted from the tag unless you are incorporating a script that uses a different scripting language. The URL of the script file must be assigned to a **src** attribute within the **<script>** tag when incorporating an external script. For example, add an adjacent script file named "script.js", like this:

<script src="script.js"> </script>

JavaScript language consists of some common programming features to be used in HTML for webpages. Common uses for JavaScript are image manipulation, form validation, and dynamic changes of content. CSS and JavaScript both are used on Web pages with HTML but for different roles. CSS is used to design the webpage for better layouts for the user, that the user can feel comfortable with the Web page. JavaScript is used to create interaction between webpages and the user.

Project 11 – Incorporating Scripts

You are going to create a JavaScript file as "script.js" in the same way as you created HTML5 document. First create a folder on desktop named **Project 11**, then write the following syntax in Notepad.

```
<!DOCTYPE HTML>
<head>

<script src="script.js"> </script>
<meta charset="UTF-8">
<title> Java </title>
</head>

<body>
<noscript> Java not enabled </noscript>
<h1> Static </h1> <h1> Dynamic </h1>
</body>
</html>
```

1. After writing this code precisely, save the file with the name "style.html" in **Project 11** folder. Make sure you type the file name in **lowercase** as mentioned, and set Encoding always as UTF-8.

2. Open **another** Notepad window and write the script code to incorporate with HTML document as mentioned below.

```
function init()
{
var h1tags = document.getElementsByTagName("h1") ; h1tags[1].onclick = react ;
}

function react()
{
this.innerHTML = "Clicked!" ; this.style.color = "red" ;
}
onload = init ;
```

3. Save this JavaScript file with the name "script.js" in the same **Project 11** folder. Make sure you type the file name in **lowercase** as mentioned, and set Encoding always as UTF-8.

4. Open the first file **script.html** in your web browser. When it is open, click on the word "**Dynamic**" in the webpage, and you will see it showing "Clicked" with the color changed to **red**.

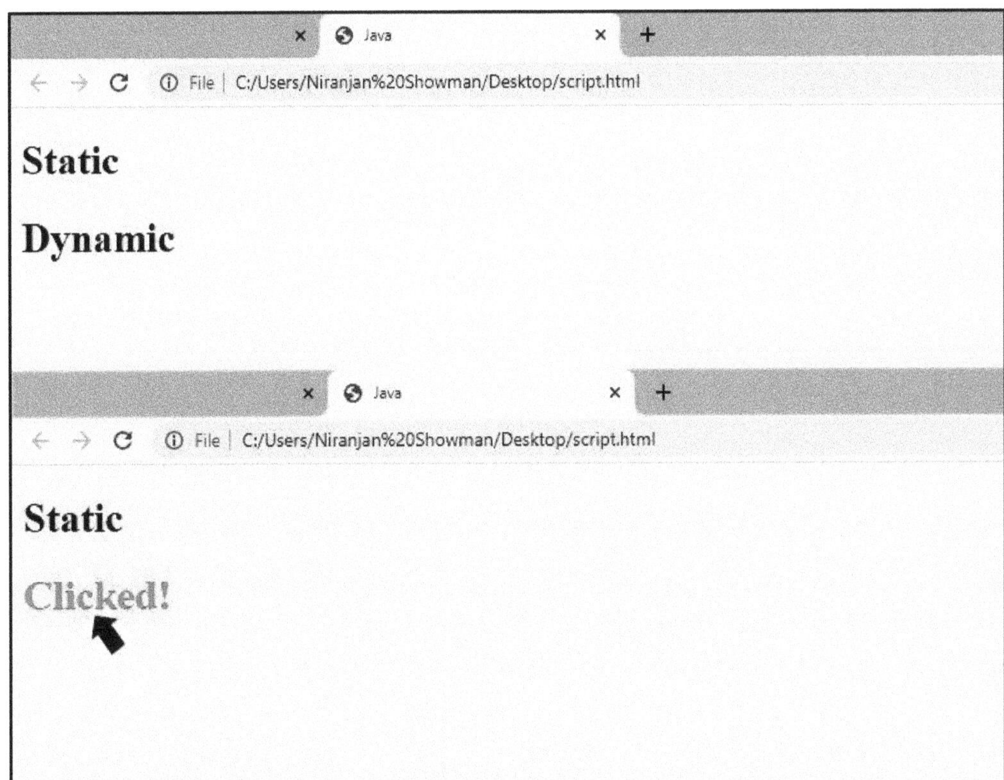

Picture 2.12: The result of incorporating scripts.

Never copy-paste the syntax in the Notepad from a Word or PDF file. You can learn more about JavaScript in a JavaScript book. This script attaches a behavior to the second heading element, so when it gets clicked by the user its text content and color change.

Chapter 3

Headings, Paragraphs, Styles

HTML headings are used to define the titles and subtitles of sections on a webpage. They help organize the content and create a structure that is easy to navigate. Proper use of headings enhances readability by organizing content into clear sections. Search engines utilize headings to understand page structure, aiding in SEO. **HTML Paragraph** is simply a block of text enclosed within the <p> tag. The <p> tag helps divide content into manageable, readable sections. This element is for wrapping text in a web page that is meant to be displayed as a distinct paragraph. **HTML Style** is used to change or add the style on existing HTML elements. There is a default style for every HTML element e.g. background color is white, text color is black etc. The style attribute can by used with any HTML tag. To apply style on HTML tag, you should have basic knowledge of css properties e.g. color, background-color, text-align, font-family, font-size etc.

1. HTML Headings

An HTML heading or HTML "h" tag can be defined as a title or a subtitle which you want to display on the webpage. When you place the text within the heading tags, it is displayed on the browser in the bold format and size of the text depends on the number of heading.

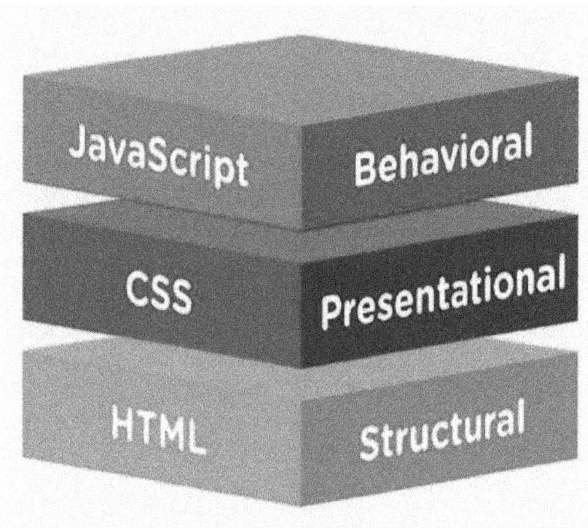

Project 12 – Bigger Headings

Each HTML heading has a default size. However, you can specify the size for any heading with the style attribute, using the CSS font-size property.

```
<!DOCTYPE html>
<html>
<body>

<h1 style="font-size:60px;">Heading 1</h1>

<p>You can change the size of a heading with the style attribute, using the font-size property.</p>

</body>
</html>
```

Picture 3.1: The result of bigger headings.

2. HTML Paragraphs

In HTML, paragraphs are defined with the tag <p>. A paragraph element in an HTML document is made up of content such as text, images, or other content like form fields that appears between an opening <p> tag and closing </p> tag. Paragraphs belong to the class of elements called block-level elements.

Project 13 – HTML Paragraphs

A paragraph always starts on a new line, and is usually a block of text. The HTML <p> element defines a paragraph. You should know that a paragraph always starts on a new line, and browsers automatically add some white space (a margin) before and after a paragraph.

```
<!DOCTYPE html>
<html>
<body>

<p>This is a paragraph.</p>

<p>This is a paragraph.</p>
<p>This is a paragraph.</p>

</body>
</html>
```

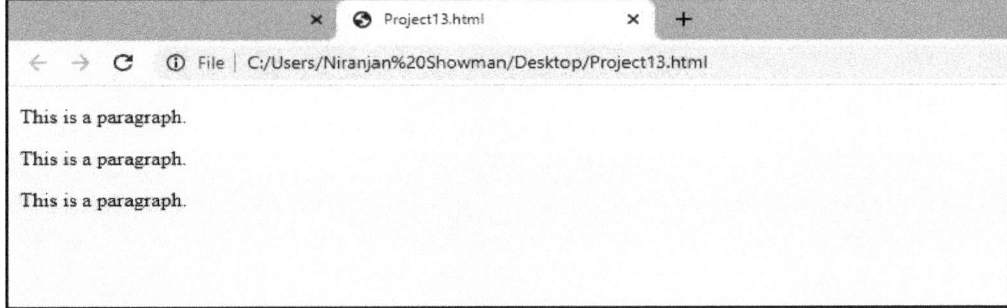

Picture 3.2: The result of HTML paragraphs.

Project 14 – HTML Display

Large or small screens, and resized windows create different results on screen. With HTML, you cannot change the display by adding extra spaces or extra lines in your HTML code. The browser will automatically remove any extra spaces and lines when the page is displayed.

```
<!DOCTYPE html>
<html>
<body>

<p>
This paragraph
contains a lot of lines
in the source code,
but the browser
ignores it.
</p>

<p>
This paragraph
contains     a lot of spaces
in the source     code,
but the   browser
ignores it.
</p>

<p>
The number of lines in a paragraph depends on the size of the browser window. If you resize the browser window, the number of lines in this paragraph will change.
</p>

</body>
</html>
```

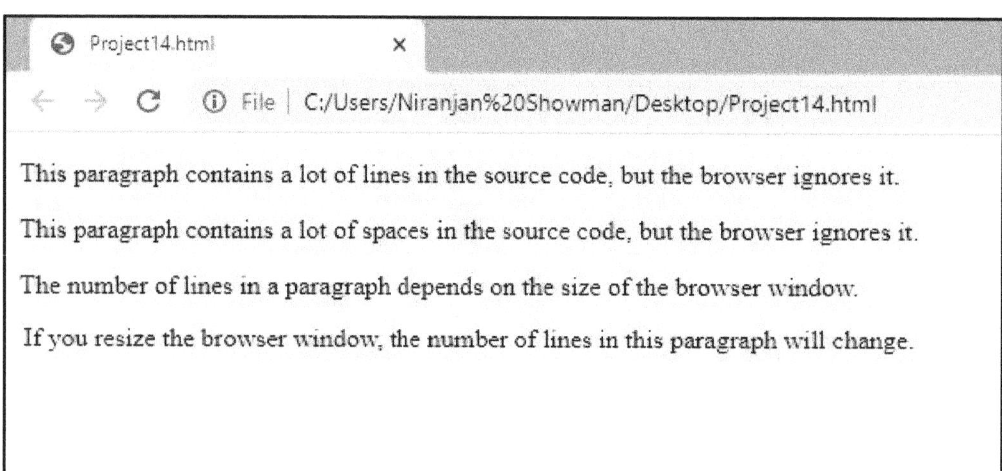

Picture 3.3: The result of HTML display.

Project 15 – HTML Horizontal Rules

The <hr> tag defines a thematic break in an HTML page, and is most often displayed as a horizontal rule. And the <hr> element is used to separate content (or define a change) in an HTML page. The <hr> tag is an empty tag, which means that it has no end tag.

```
<!DOCTYPE html>
<html>
<body>

<h1>This is heading 1</h1>
<p>This is some text.</p>
<hr>

<h2>This is heading 2</h2>
<p>This is some other text.</p>
<hr>

<h2>This is heading 2</h2>
<p>This is some other text.</p>

</body>
</html>
```

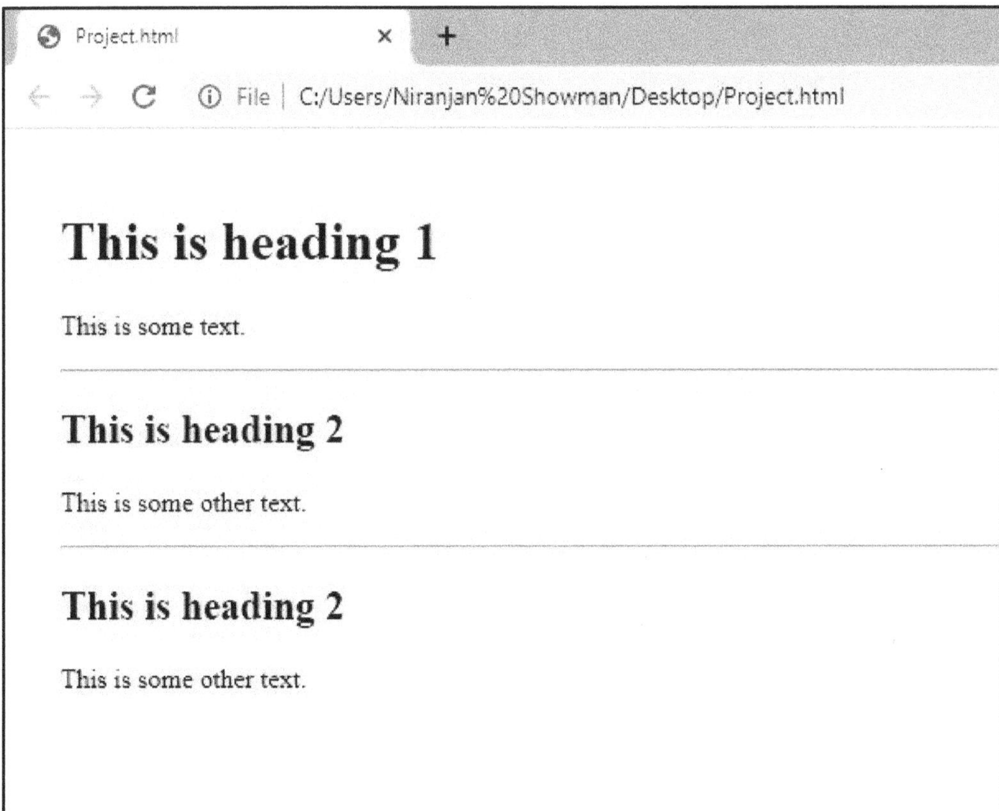

Picture 3.4: The result of HTML horizontal rules.

Project 16 – HTML Line Breaks

The HTML <br> element defines a line break. Use <br> if you want a line break (a new line) without starting a new paragraph. The <br> tag is an empty tag, which means that it has no end tag.

```
<!DOCTYPE html>
<html>
<body>

<p>This is<br>a paragraph<br>with line breaks.</p>

</body>
</html>
```

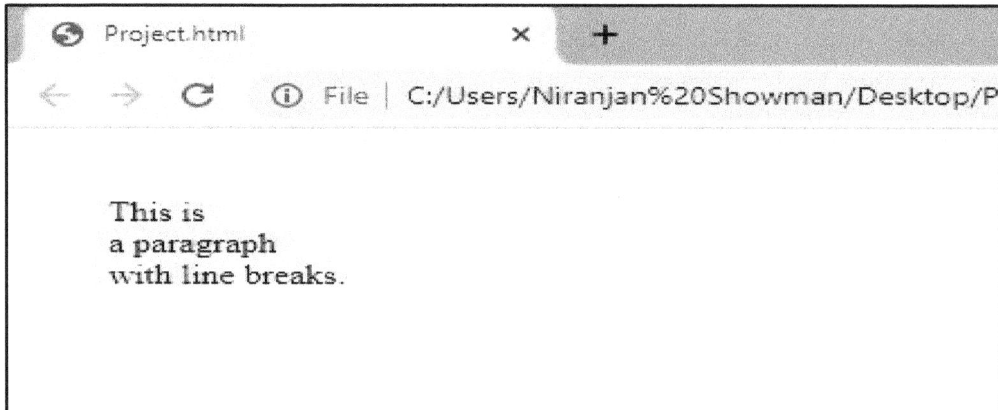

Picture 3.5: The result of HTML line breaks.

Project 17 – The Poem Problem

The Poem Problem is a situation in HTML when you want to a "line break" after every verse of your poem, but the <p> tag ignores spaces and new lines. The entire poem will be displayed on a single line which is definitely **not** what you want.

```
<!DOCTYPE html>
<html>
<body>

<p>The pre tag preserves both spaces and line breaks:</p>

<pre>
  My Bonnie lies over the ocean.
  My Bonnie lies over the sea.
  My Bonnie lies over the ocean.
  Oh, bring back my Bonnie to me.
</pre>

</body>
</html>
```

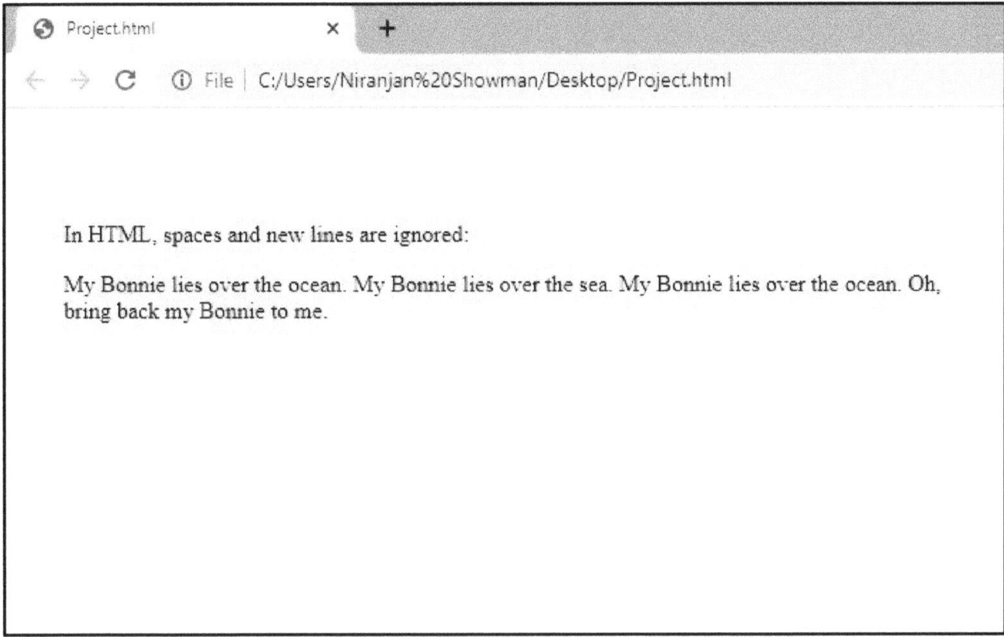

Picture 3.6: The result of poem problem.

Project 18 – Solution To Poem Problem

The HTML <pre> tag defines preformatted text. The text inside a <pre> element is displayed in a fixed-width font (usually Courier), and it preserves both spaces and line breaks. The code written below will solve the problem that you faced in previous project.

```
<!DOCTYPE html>
<html>
<body>

<p>The pre tag preserves both spaces and line breaks:</p>

<pre>
  My Bonnie lies over the ocean.

  My Bonnie lies over the sea.

  My Bonnie lies over the lake.

  My Bonnie lies over the ocean.

  Oh, bring back my Bonnie to me.
</pre>

</body>
</html>
```

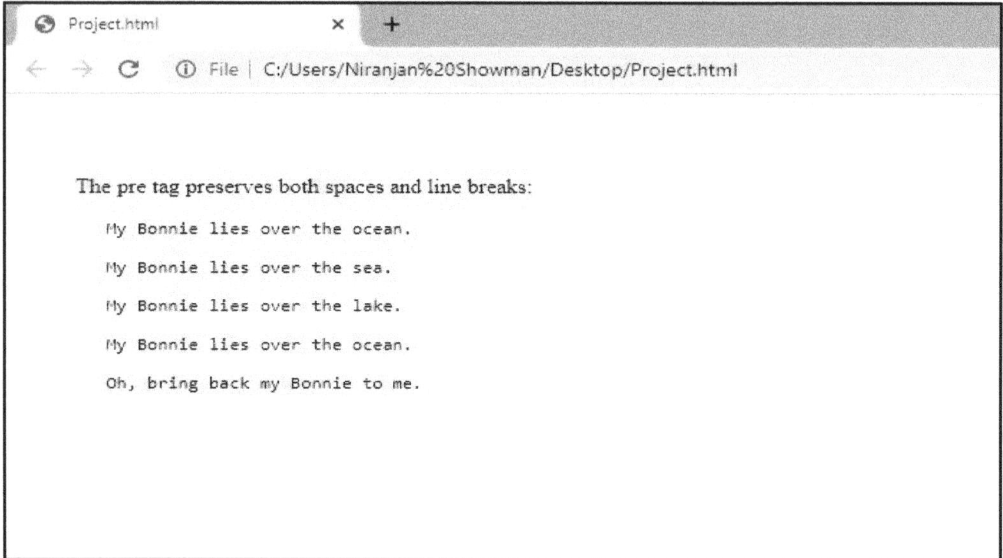

Picture 3.7: The solution to poem problem.

3. HTML Styles

HTML Style is used to change or add the style on existing HTML elements. There is a default style for every HTML element e.g. background color is white, text color is black etc. The style attribute can by used with any HTML tag. To apply style on HTML tag, you should have the basic knowledge of css properties e.g. color, background-color, text-align, font-family, font-size etc.

The HTML **style** attribute has the following syntax in which, the property is a CSS **property**, and the **value** is a CSS value:

<tagname style="property:value;">

Project 19 – HTML Styles

The HTML style attribute is used to add styles to an element, such as color, font, size, and more. Setting the style of an HTML element, can be done with the **style** attribute.

```
<!DOCTYPE html>
<html>
<body>

<p>I am normal</p>
<p style="color:red;">I am red</p>
<p style="color:blue;">I am blue</p>
<p style="font-size:50px;">I am big</p>

</body>
</html>
```

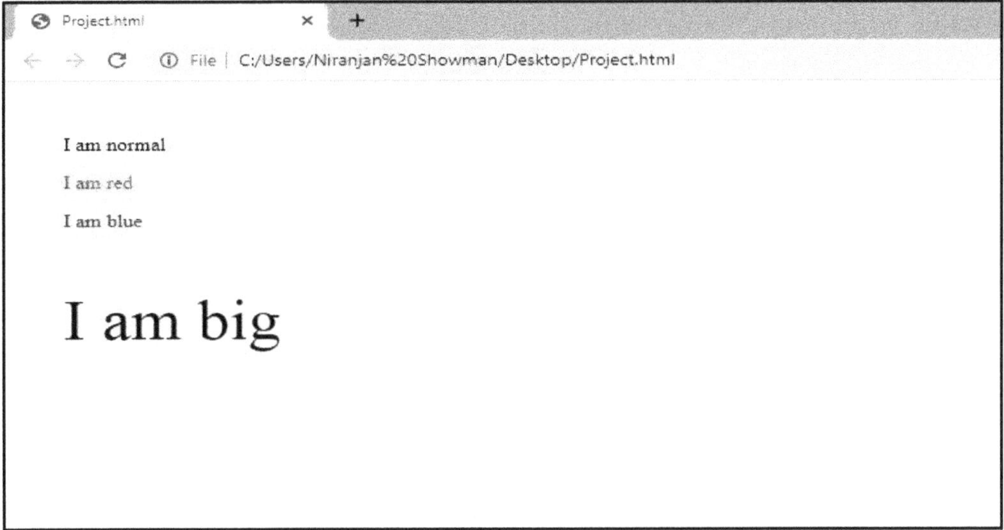

Picture 3.8: The result of HTML styles.

Project 20 – Background Color

The CSS background color property defines the background color for an HTML element. We are going to set the background color for a page to powderblue.

```
<!DOCTYPE html>
<html>
<body style="background-color:powderblue;">

<h1>This is a heading</h1>
<p>This is a paragraph.</p>

</body>
</html>
```

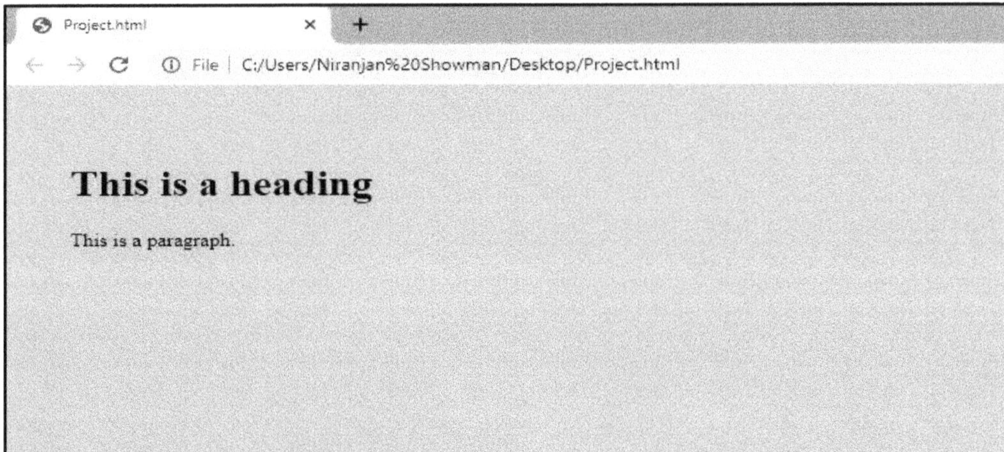

Picture 3.9: The result of background color.

Project 21 – Background Color For Two Elements

In this project we are going to set background color for two different elements. Here is the code that you need to write precisely.

```
<!DOCTYPE html>
<html>
<body>

<h1 style="background-color:powderblue;">This is a heading</h1>
<p style="background-color:tomato;">This is a paragraph.</p>

</body>
</html>
```

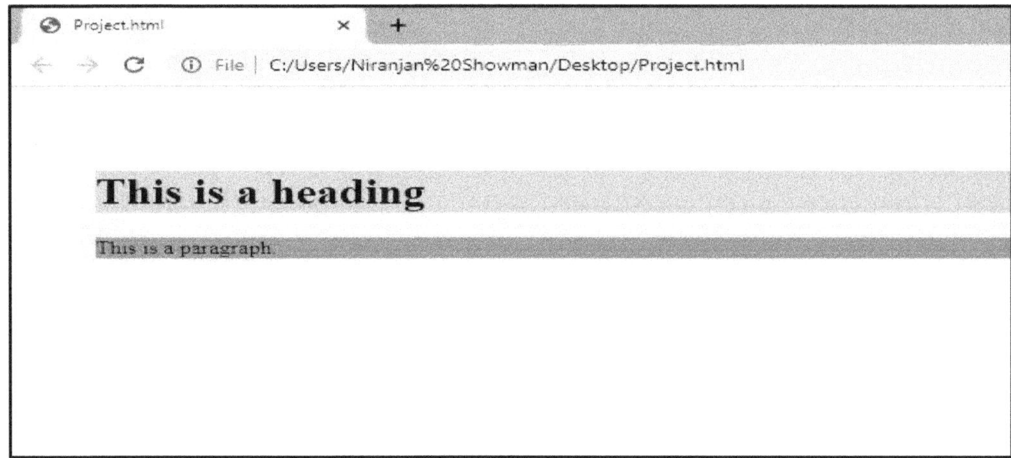

Picture 3.10: Background color for two elements.

Project 22 – Text Color And Font Style

The CSS color property defines the text color for an HTML element. And the CSS font-family property defines the font to be used for an HTML element.

```
<!DOCTYPE html>
<html>
<body>

<h1 style="color:blue;">This is a heading</h1>
<h1 style="font-family:verdana;">This is a heading</h1>

<p style="color:red;">This is a paragraph.</p>
<p style="font-family:courier;">This is a paragraph.</p>

</body>
</html>
```

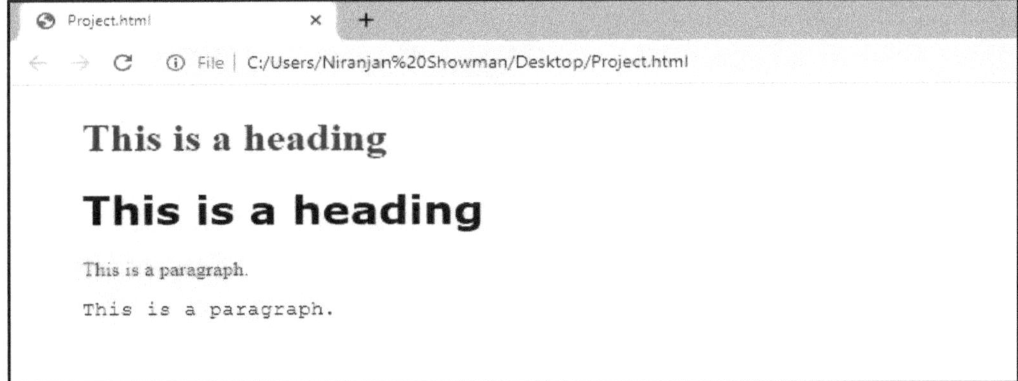

Picture 3.11: Text color and font style.

Project 23 – Text Size And Text Alignment

The CSS font-size property defines the text size for an HTML element. And the CSS text-align property defines the horizontal text alignment for an HTML element.

```
<!DOCTYPE html>
<html>
<body>

<h1 style="font-size:300%;">
<h1 style="text-align:center;">
Centered Heading
</h1>

<p style="font-size:160%;">
<p style="text-align:center;">
This is a paragraph
</p>

</body>
</html>
```

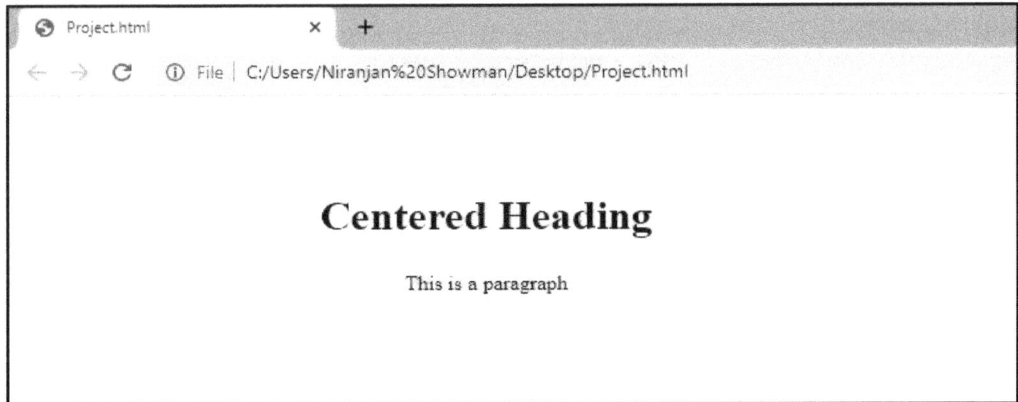

Picture 3.12: Text size and text alignment.

Chapter 4

Creating Body Content

An HTML5 webpage needs the body content to be created. This section of the chapter demonstrates how text and image elements can be created within the body section of an HTML5 document. In this section, you will learn: Emphasizing text, Marking text, and Working the body.

1. Emphasizing Text

While learning to emphasing texts, you need to understand phrasing elements. HTML provides four phrasing elements that can be used to emphasize text within the body of a document:

- Text enclosed between **<b> </b>** tags is enhanced without conveying extra importance, such as keywords in a paragraph – typically displayed in a bold font.

- Text enclosed between **<i> </i>** tags is enhanced without conveying extra importance, such as technical terms in a paragraph – typically displayed in an italic font.

- Text enhanced between **<strong> </strong>** tags gains increased importance, without changing the meaning of the sentence – typically displayed in a bold font.

- Text enclosed between **<em> </em>** tags should be stressed to deliberately affect the meaning of the sentence – typically displayed in an italic font.

Project 24 – Emphasizing Text

The **<b> and <i>** tags in HTML5 suggest to the web that the content should be presented in a bold or italic font – contradicting the aim of HTML5 to separate structure from presentation. According to the specifications, their meaning has been redefined, however, so content within a **<b>** element should be "stylistically offset" and that within an **<i>** element should be seen as in an "alternate aspect".

```
<!DOCTYPE html>
<html>
<head>

<meta charset="UTF-8">
<title> Emphasis Example </title>
</head>

<body>
<p> <strong> Warning. </strong> This dungeon is dangerous. <strong> Avoid the ducks. </strong> Take
any gold you find. </p>
<p> <em> Puppy dogs </em> are cute. </P>
<p> Puppy dogs <em> are </em>  cute. </P>
<p> Puppy dogs are <em> cute. </em> </P>

</body>
</html>
```

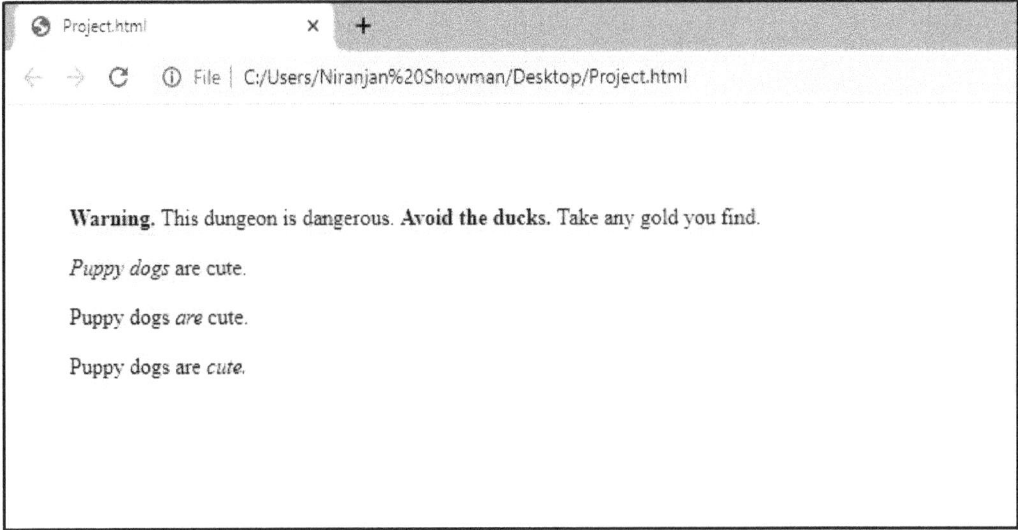

Picture 4.1: The result of emphasing text.

The advantage of the **<strong>** and **<em>** tags in HTML5 is that they describe the importance of their content relative to surrounding text, and they let the browser choose how it should be presented. Additionally, these tags are more relevant to suggest how narrators should convey their content vocally. As with many HTML tags, the **<strong>** and **<em>** tags can be nested, but care must be taken to close nested elements correctly. For example, **<strong> <em> … </em> </strong>** is the correct order, whereas **<strong> <em> … </strong> </em>** is incorrect and will not validate.

Example Explained: -

- The **<p> <strong> Warning. </strong>** element within the body section, add a paragraph that emphasizes some text without affecting the meaning of the sentences.
- The <p> <em> Puppy dogs </em> element within the body section, add paragraph that emphasize some text to affect the meaning of the sentence.

2. Reading Small Print

HTML5 provides three elements that can be used to format text within the body of a document. Here is the detail of those three elements"

- Text enclosed between **<small> </small>** tags is regarded as a side comment to surrounding text, such as copyright information – typically displayed in a smaller font.

- Text enclosed within **<del> </del>** tags is regarded as having been removed from the document, such as a completed item in a to-do list – typically displayed with a strike-through line.

- Text enclosed within **<ins> </ins>** tags is regarded as having been added to the document, such as a new additional item in a "to do" list – typically displayed with an underline.

Project 25 – Reading Small Print

In this project, we are going to write an HTML code that will present the text on web such as (A) smaller front, (B) strike-through, (C) underline.

```
<!DOCTYPE html>
<html>

<head>
<meta charset="UTF-8"> <title> Format Example </title>
</head>

<body>
<p> Example Corp was announced today <small> (Full Disclosure) </small> leading to speculation. </p>
<h1> To Do List </h1>
<p> Empty the dishwasher </p>
<del> <p> Take out the trash </p> </del>
<ins> <p> Sweep the yard </p> </ins>

<ins>
<p> Feed the <del>dog</del> <ins> cat </ins> </p>
</ins>

</body>
</html>
```

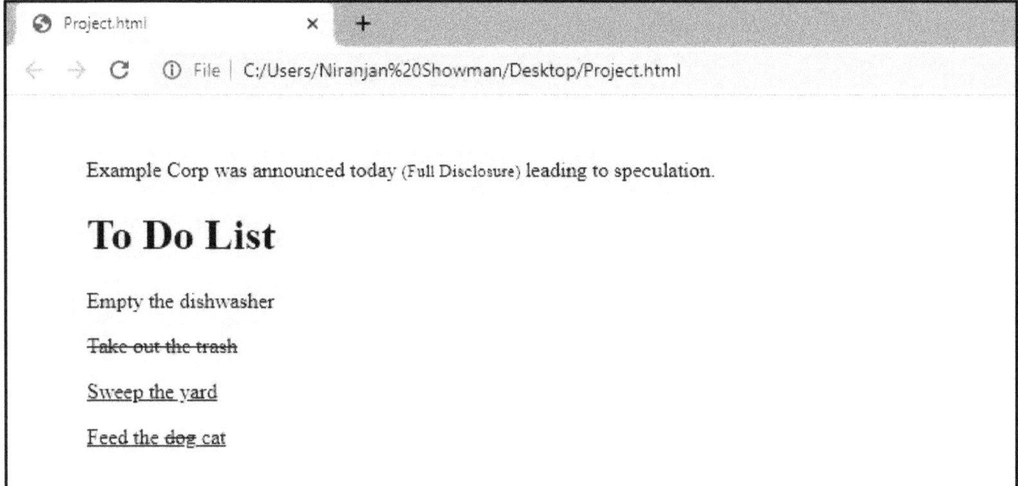

Picture 4.2: The result of reading small print.

Example Explained: -

- The **<p> Empty the dishwasher </p>** element inserts a regular paragraph.
- The **<del> <p> Take out the trash </p> </del>** deletes a paragraph with strike-through.
- The **<ins> <p> Sweep the yard </p> </ins>** element inserts a paragraph with underline.

The **<del>** and **<ins>** tags may optionally include a cite attribute to specify the URL of a document explaining the changes made. The **<small>** tag is only meant to contain short comments that supplement surrounding content. It is not intended for use with large sections of text, such as multiple paragraphs, as that would be considerable more than a side comment.

In displaying content contained within a <small> element, your web browser considers the size of the font used to display the surrounding content, then applies an appropriate reduction. Therefore, where the surrounding content is displayed with a font of 12-point size, content contained within a <small> element might be displayed with a font of 10-point size – the precise size is determined by the browser. Both <del> and <ins> elements can be used within a section of content, to mark up snippets of changed text, and to enclose entire sections of changed content, such as replaced paragraphs.

3. Marking Text

HTML5 provides four phrasing elements that can be used to mark text for special treatment within the body of a document:

- Text enclosed between **<s> </s>** tags is marked as being superseded by more accurate or relevant up-to-date content – typically displayed with a strike-through line.
- Text enclosed between **<u> </u>** tags is marked as being different in some way to normal text content – typically displayed with an underscore line to underline the text.
- Text enclosed between **<mark> </mark>** is marked as being of specific significance for the reference – typically displayed in a colored background block to highlight the text.
- Text broken by a **<wbr>** tag is invisibly marked as being a suitable point at which to break a line to text – representing word-break opportunity.

Project 26 – Marking Text

```
<!DOCTYPE html>
<html>

<head>
<meta charset="UTF-8">
<title> Mark Example </title>
</head>

<body>
<p> Microsoft Surface Pro 4
<wbr> - 128GB / Intel Core i5</p>
<p> <s>$999</s> $799</p>
<p> Memory: <mark>4GB</mark>
<br>Screen: <mark>12.3-inch</mark> </p>
<p> Surface <u>Penn</u> Included </p>

</body>
</html>
```

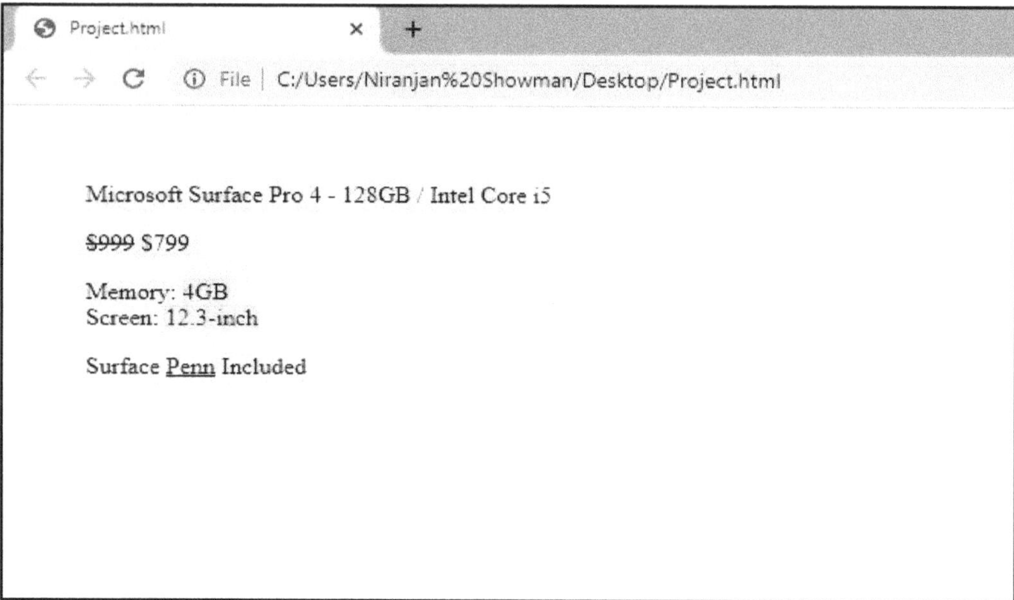

Picture 4.3: The result of marking text.

Example Explained: -

- The **<p> Microsoft Surface Pro 4** and **<wbr> - 128GB / Intel Core i5</p>** elements add a paragraph that marks a word-break.
- The **<p> <s>$999</s> $799</p>** element adds a paragraph that marks a superseded price and provides a current price.
- The **<p> Memory:** and **
Screen:** and **<p> Surface** elements add paragraphs that mark text for reference and mark a misspelled word.

The <s>, <mark>, and <wbr> tags are new elements introduced in HTML 5.1, whereas the <u> tag has been reinstalled in HTML 5.1 after previously being deprecated. Use style sheet rules for presentation purposes rather than the <u> tag for underlines.

It is important to note that specifications state that the <s> tag should not be used to indicate edited content within a document. The <del> tag should be used instead to indicate the document edits. Similarly, the <mark> tag should not be used to emphasize the importance of text content, but should only be used to highlight the relevance of text within a document. The <strong> and <em> tags should be used instead to indicate emphasis.

The <u> was deprecated in the HTML 5.0 specification, as underlined text within a document traditionally indicates hyperlinks. The <u> tag has, however, reappeared in the HTML 5.1 specification for the purpose of labeling misspelled words. Authors are nonetheless strongly discouraged from using the <u> tag for emphasis, to avoid confusion with hyperlinks. Once again, the <strong> and <em> tags should be used instead to indicate emphasis. Where the document contains lengthy content that may exceed the width of the browser, you may wish to use the <wbr> tag to indicate appropriate points at which a line-break can be inserted.

Project 27 – Text Formatting

HTML contains several elements for defining text with a special meaning. This project explains how to make subscript and superscript text.

```
<!DOCTYPE html>
<html>
<body>

<p><b>This text is bold</b></p>
<p><i>This text is italic</i></p>
<p>This is<sub> subscript</sub> and <sup>superscript</sup></p>

</body>
</html>
```

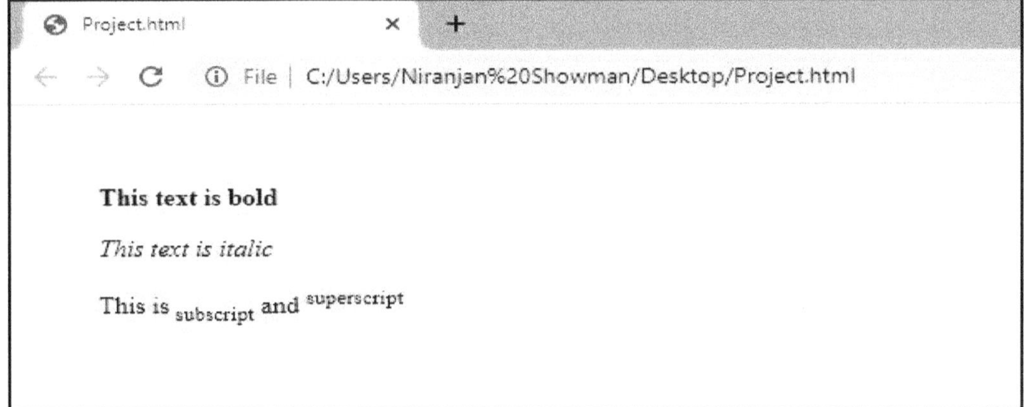

Picture 4.4: The result of text formatting.

HTML Text Formatting Elements

Tag	Description
<b>	Defines bold text
<em>	Defines emphasized text
<i>	Defines a part of text in an alternate voice or mood
<small>	Defines smaller text
<strong>	Defines important text
<sub>	Defines subscripted text
<sup>	Defines superscripted text
<ins>	Defines inserted text
<del>	Defines deleted text
<mark>	Defines marked/highlighted text

Project 28 – HTML Comment Tag

HTML comments are not displayed in the browser, but they can help document your HTML source code. You can add comments to your HTML source by using the following syntax. Notice that there is an exclamation point **(!)** in the start tag, but not in the end tag. With comments you can place notifications and reminders in your HTML code.

```
<!DOCTYPE html>
<html>
<body>

<!-- This is a comment -->
<p>This is a paragraph.</p>
<!-- Comments are not displayed in the browser -->

</body>
</html>
```

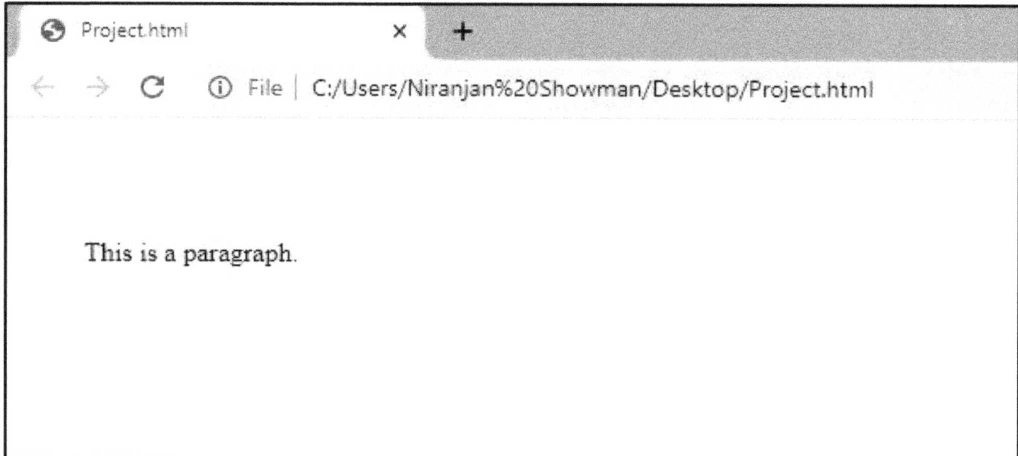

Picture 4.5: The result of comment tag.

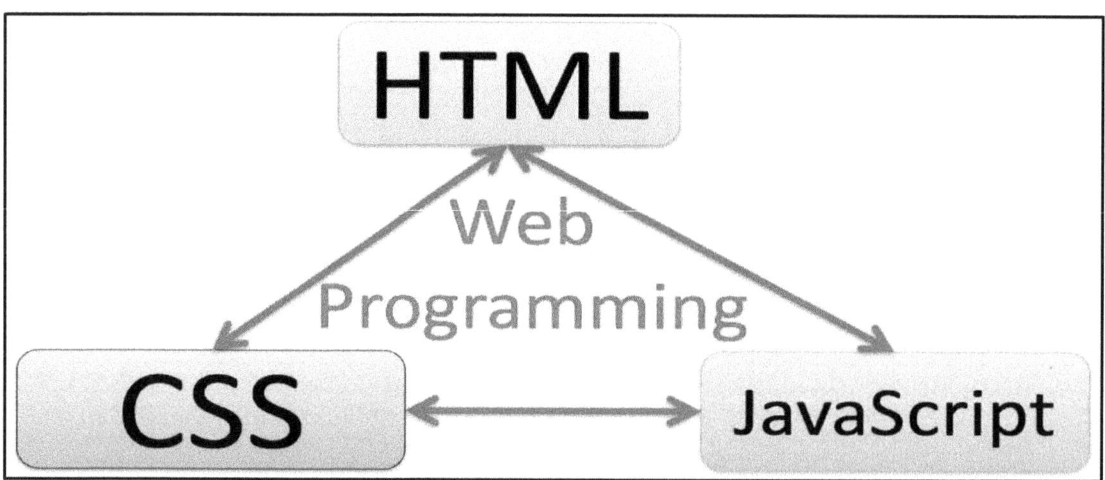

HTML5 Advanced

Chapter 5

HTML Colors

HTML colors are specified with predefined color names, or with RGB, HEX, HSL, RGBA, or HSLA values. In HTML, a color can be specified by using a color name.

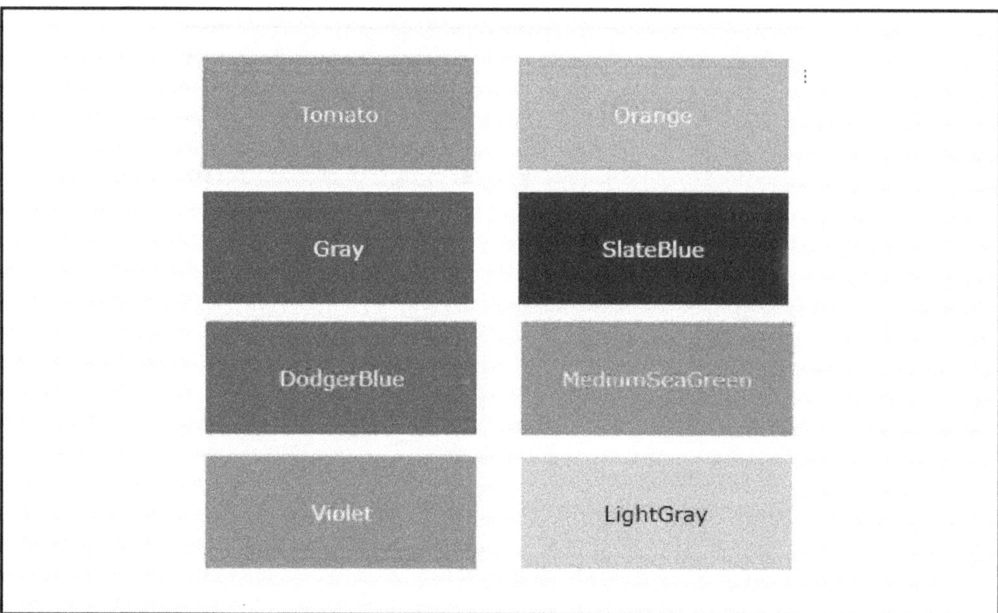

Project 29 – Naming Colors

It is necessary to mention that HTML supports 140 standard color names. In HTML, a color can be specified by using a color name

```
<!DOCTYPE html>
<html>
<body>

<h1 style="background-color:Tomato;">Tomato</h1>
<h1 style="background-color:Orange;">Orange</h1>
<h1 style="background-color:DodgerBlue;">DodgerBlue</h1>
<h1 style="background-color:MediumSeaGreen;">MediumSeaGreen</h1>
<h1 style="background-color:Gray;">Gray</h1>
<h1 style="background-color:SlateBlue;">SlateBlue</h1>
<h1 style="background-color:Violet;">Violet</h1>
<h1 style="background-color:LightGray;">LightGray</h1>

</body>
</html>
```

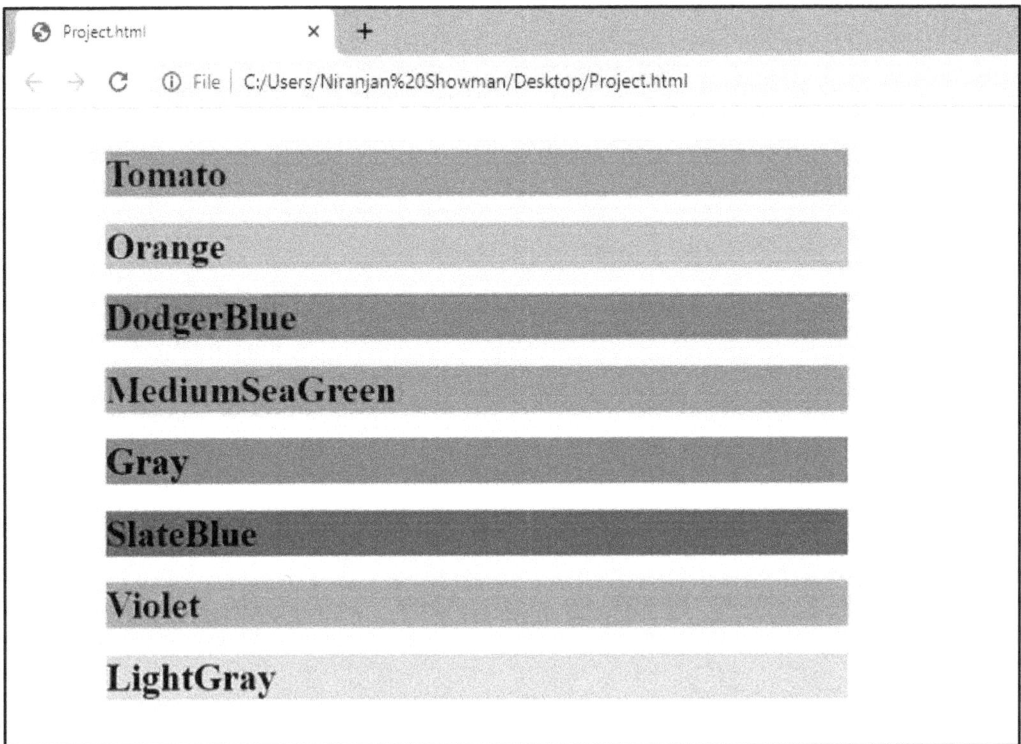

Picture 5.1: The result of naming colors.

Project 30 – Background Color

You can set the background color for HTML elements. You can use the style attribute to specify the background color for the HTML element and then set the value using the background-color property. The background-color property accepts color names, RGB, RGBA, HEX, HSL, or HSLA values. You need to determine which element you want to change the background color for. If it's a paragraph, look for the <p> opening tag. It can also be an <h1>...<h6>, <div> or <table> tag.

```
<!DOCTYPE html>
<html>
<body>

<h1 style="background-color:DodgerBlue;">Hello World</h1>

<p style="background-color:Tomato;">
Lorem ipsum dolor sit amet, consectetuer adipiscing elit, sed diam nonummy nibh euismod tincidunt ut laoreet dolore magna aliquam erat volutpat.
Ut wisi enim ad minim veniam, quis nostrud exerci tation ullamcorper suscipit lobortis nisl ut aliquip ex ea commodo consequat.
</p>

</body>
</html>
```

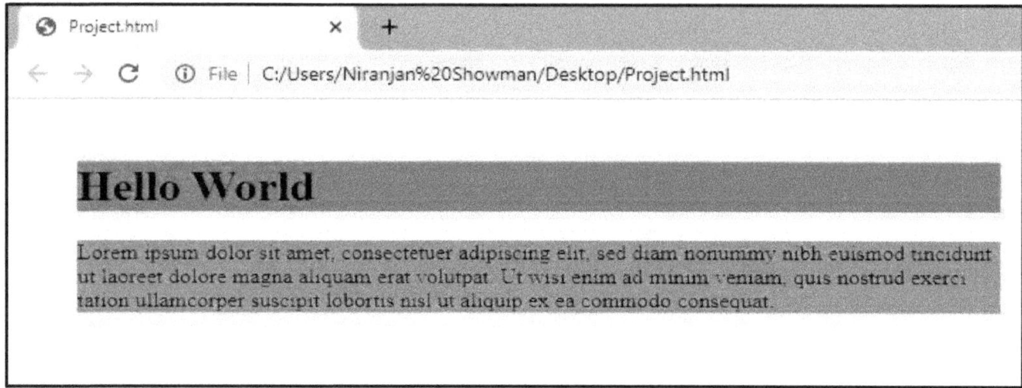

Picture 5.2: The result of background color.

Project 31 – Text Color

Here we are going to set the color of text. You can use the inline style attribute or the <style> element to change the text color and then set the value using the color property.

```
<!DOCTYPE html>
<html>
<body>

<h3 style="color:Tomato;">Hello World</h3>

<p style="color:DodgerBlue;">Lorem ipsum dolor sit amet, consectetuer adipiscing elit, sed diam nonummy nibh euismod tincidunt ut laoreet dolore magna aliquam erat volutpat.</p>

<p style="color:MediumSeaGreen;">Ut wisi enim ad minim veniam, quis nostrud exerci tation ullamcorper suscipit lobortis nisl ut aliquip ex ea commodo consequat.</p>

</body>
</html>
```

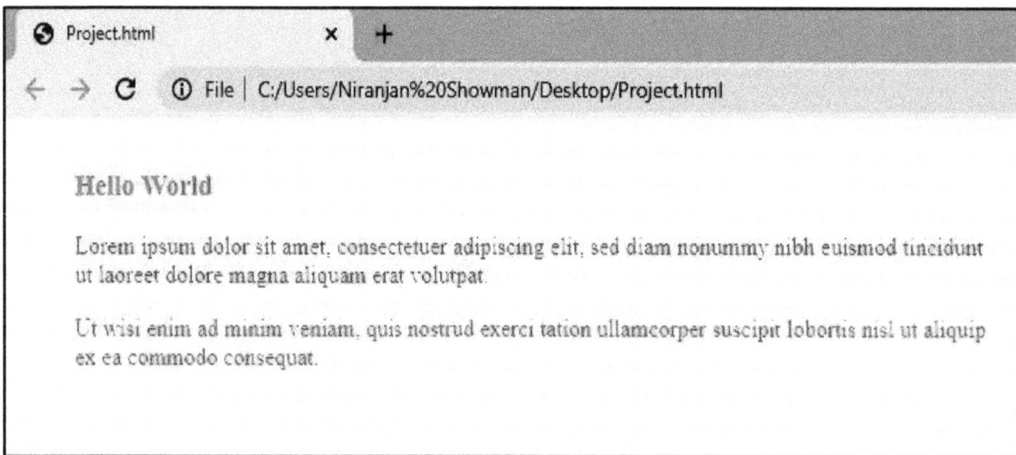

Picture 5.3: The result of text color.

Project 32 – Border Color

You can set the color of borders using inline **style** attribute. Adding color to a web page is a part of inline CSS styling. To set the border, text or background color in HTML, you need to use the style attribute.

```
<!DOCTYPE html>
<html>
<body>

<h1 style="border: 2px solid Tomato;">Hello World</h1>

<h1 style="border: 2px solid DodgerBlue;">Hello World</h1>

<h1 style="border: 2px solid Violet;">Hello World</h1>

</body>
</html>
```

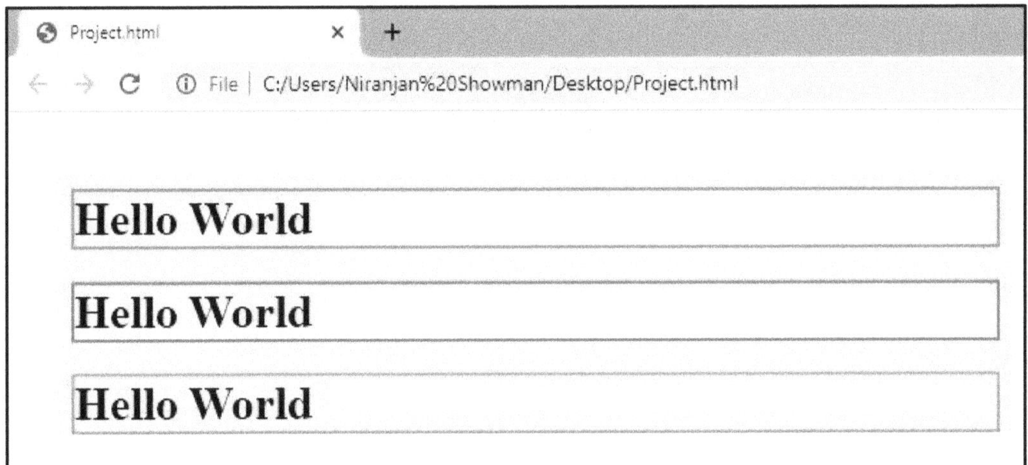

Picture 5.4: The result of border color.

Project 33 – RGB Color Values

An **RGB** color value represents RED, GREEN, and BLUE light sources. An **RGBA** color value is an extension of RGB with an Alpha channel (opacity). In HTML, a color can be specified as an RGB value, using rgb(red, green, blue) formula.

- Each parameter (red, green, and blue) defines intensity of color with a value between 0 and 255.
- This means that there are 256 x 256 x 256 = 16777216 possible colors!
- For example, rgb(255, 0, 0) is displayed as red, because red is set to its highest value (255), and the other two (green and blue) are set to 0.
- Another example, rgb(0, 255, 0) is displayed as green, because green is set to its highest value (255), and the other two (red and blue) are set to 0.
- To display black, set all color parameters to 0, like this: rgb(0, 0, 0).
- To display white, set all color parameters to 255, like this: rgb(255, 255, 255).

```html
<!DOCTYPE html>
<html>
<body>

<h1 style="background-color:rgb(255, 0, 0);">rgb(255, 0, 0)</h1>
<h1 style="background-color:rgb(0, 0, 255);">rgb(0, 0, 255)</h1>
<h1 style="background-color:rgb(60, 179, 113);">rgb(60, 179, 113)</h1>
<h1 style="background-color:rgb(238, 130, 238);">rgb(238, 130, 238)</h1>
<h1 style="background-color:rgb(255, 165, 0);">rgb(255, 165, 0)</h1>
<h1 style="background-color:rgb(106, 90, 205);">rgb(106, 90, 205)</h1>

</body>
</html>
```

Picture 5.5: The result of RGB color values.

Project 34 – Shades of Gray

Shades of gray are often defined using equal values for all three parameters.

```html
<!DOCTYPE html>
<html>
<body>

<h1 style="background-color:rgb(60, 60, 60);">rgb(60, 60, 60)</h1>
<h1 style="background-color:rgb(100, 100, 100);">rgb(100, 100, 100)</h1>
<h1 style="background-color:rgb(140, 140, 140);">rgb(140, 140, 140)</h1>
<h1 style="background-color:rgb(180, 180, 180);">rgb(180, 180, 180)</h1>
<h1 style="background-color:rgb(200, 200, 200);">rgb(200, 200, 200)</h1>
<h1 style="background-color:rgb(240, 240, 240);">rgb(240, 240, 240)</h1>

</body>
</html>
```

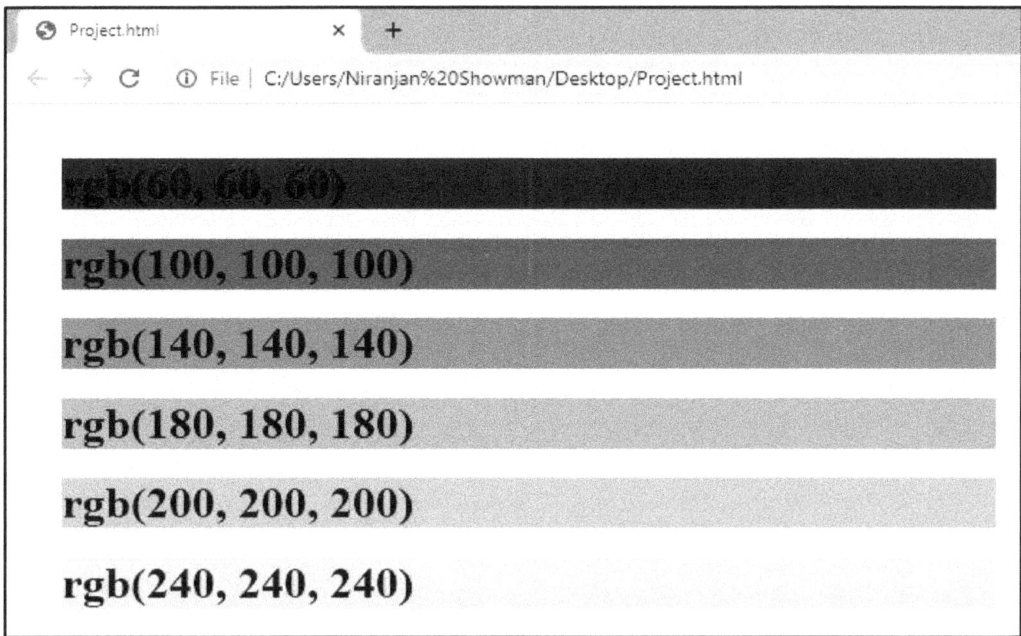

Picture 5.6: The result of shades of gray.

Shades of gray consist of both achromatic grayscale shades, which are varying combinations of black and white, and close colors that have very low saturation. Achromatic grays include shades like gainsboro and silver, with no saturation at all, while grayish colors include taupe, ash, and cadet gray.

Project 35 – HSL Color Values

HSL stands for hue, saturation, and lightness. In HTML, a color can be specified using hue, saturation, and lightness (HSL) in the form: hsl(hue, saturation, lightness). Hue is a degree on the color wheel from 0 to 360. 0 is red, 120 is green, and 240 is blue. Saturation is a percentage value. 0% means a shade of gray, and 100% is the full color. Lightness is also a percentage value. 0% is black, and 100% is white. You can experiment by mixing the HSL values below.

```
<!DOCTYPE html>
<html>
<body>

<h1 style="background-color:hsl(0, 100%, 50%);">hsl(0, 100%, 50%)</h1>
<h1 style="background-color:hsl(240, 100%, 50%);">hsl(240, 100%, 50%)</h1>
<h1 style="background-color:hsl(147, 50%, 47%);">hsl(147, 50%, 47%)</h1>
<h1 style="background-color:hsl(300, 76%, 72%);">hsl(300, 76%, 72%)</h1>
<h1 style="background-color:hsl(39, 100%, 50%);">hsl(39, 100%, 50%)</h1>
<h1 style="background-color:hsl(248, 53%, 58%);">hsl(248, 53%, 58%)</h1>

</body>
</html>
```

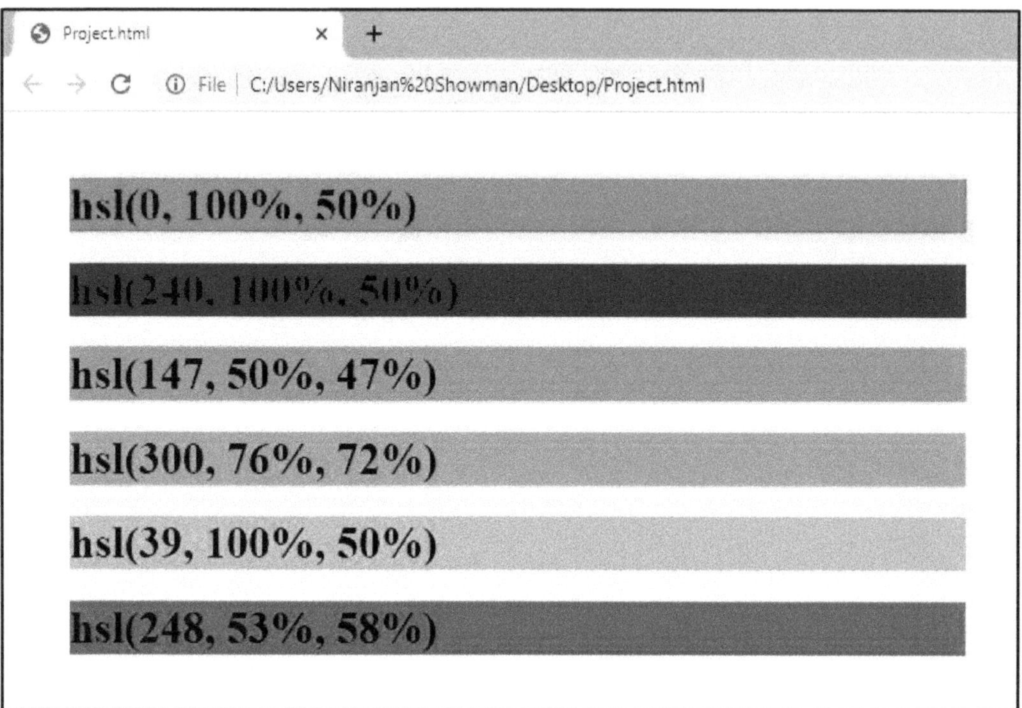

Picture 5.7: The result of HSL color values.

Project 36 – Color Saturation

Saturation can be described as the intensity of a color. 100% is pure color with no shades of gray. 50% is 50% gray, but you can still see the color. 0% is completely gray; you can no longer see the color. Whereas the lightness of a color can be described as how much light you want to give the color, where 0% means no light (black), 50% means 50% light (neither dark nor light), and 100% means full lightness (white). The code mentioned below describes the color saturation.

```
<!DOCTYPE html>
<html>
<body>

<h1 style="background-color:hsl(0, 100%, 50%);">hsl(0, 100%, 50%)</h1>
<h1 style="background-color:hsl(0, 80%, 50%);">hsl(0, 80%, 50%)</h1>
<h1 style="background-color:hsl(0, 60%, 50%);">hsl(0, 60%, 50%)</h1>
<h1 style="background-color:hsl(0, 40%, 50%);">hsl(0, 40%, 50%)</h1>
<h1 style="background-color:hsl(0, 20%, 50%);">hsl(0, 20%, 50%)</h1>
<h1 style="background-color:hsl(0, 0%, 50%);">hsl(0, 0%, 50%)</h1>

<p>With HSL colors, less saturation mean less color. 0% is completely gray.</p>

</body>
</html>
```

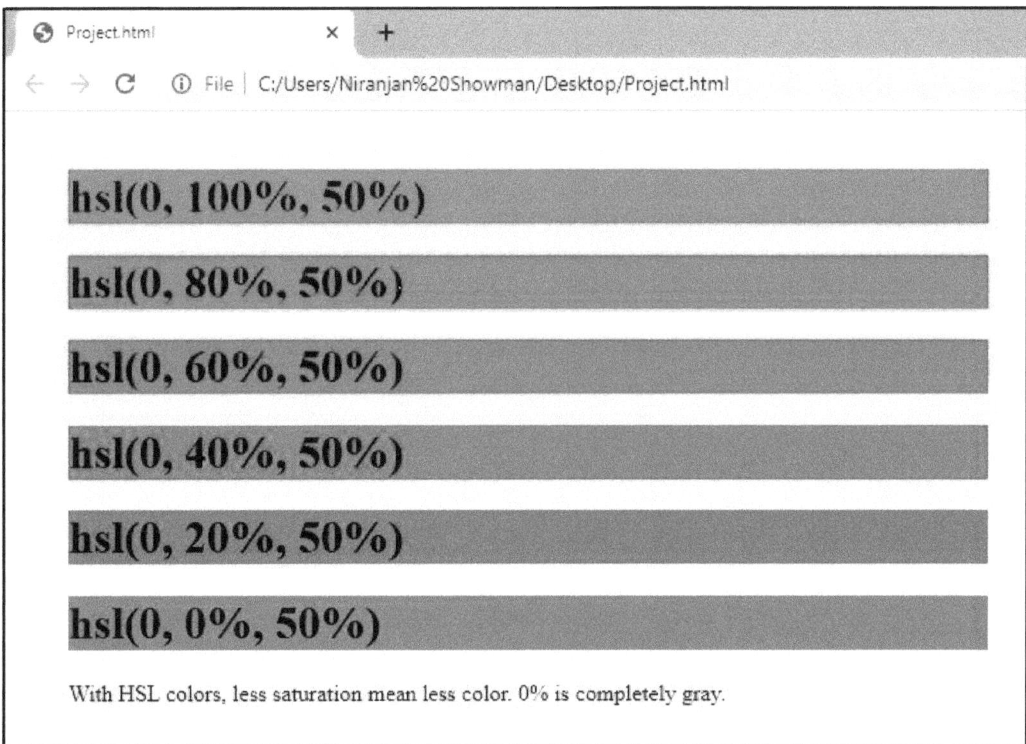

Picture 5.8: The result of color saturation.

In the next chapter, you will learn in detail how to add CSS to an HTML document. The very first thing we need to do is to tell the HTML document that we have some CSS rules we want it to use. There are three different ways to apply CSS to an HTML document that you'll commonly come across — external stylesheets, internal stylesheets, and inline styles. Let's look at these in the next chapter.

Chapter 6

HTML CSS, HTML JavaScript

CSS stands for Cascading Style Sheets. It can control the layout of multiple web pages all at once. CSS is used to format the layout of a webpage. With CSS, you can control the color, font, and size of text. You can also manage spaces between elements, their positions, background images, background colors, and provide different displays for different devices and screen sizes, and much more!

1. Using CSS

The word cascading means that a style applied to a parent element will also apply to all children elements within the parent. So, if you set the color of the body text to "blue", all headings, paragraphs, and other text elements within the body will also get the same color (unless you specify something else). CSS can be added to HTML documents in 3 ways:

- **Inline** - by using the style attribute inside HTML elements
- **Internal** - by using a <style> element in the <head> section
- **External** - by using a <link> element to link to an external CSS file

The most common way to add CSS, is to keep the styles in external CSS files. However, in this chapter we will use inline and internal styles, because this is easier to demonstrate, and easier for you to try.

Project 37 – Inline CSS

```
<!DOCTYPE html>
<html>
<body>

<h1 style="color:blue;">A Blue Heading</h1>

<p style="color:red;">A red paragraph.</p>

</body>
</html>
```

Picture 6.1: The result of Inline CSS.

In project 37 above, we used **Inline** CSS code to apply a unique style to a single HTML element. An inline CSS uses the **style** attribute of an HTML element. The following example sets the text color of the <h1> element to blue, and the text color of the <p> element to red.

Project 38 – Internal CSS

An internal CSS is used to define a style for a single HTML page. An internal CSS is defined in the <head> section of an HTML page, within a <style> element. The following example sets the text color of ALL the <h1> elements (on that page) to blue, and the text color of ALL the <p> elements to red. In addition, the page will be displayed with a "powderblue" background color.

```
<!DOCTYPE html>
<html>
<head>

<style>
body {background-color: powderblue;}
h1   {color: blue;}
p    {color: red;}
</style>
</head>
<body>

<h1>This is a heading</h1>
<p>This is a paragraph.</p>

</body>
</html>
```

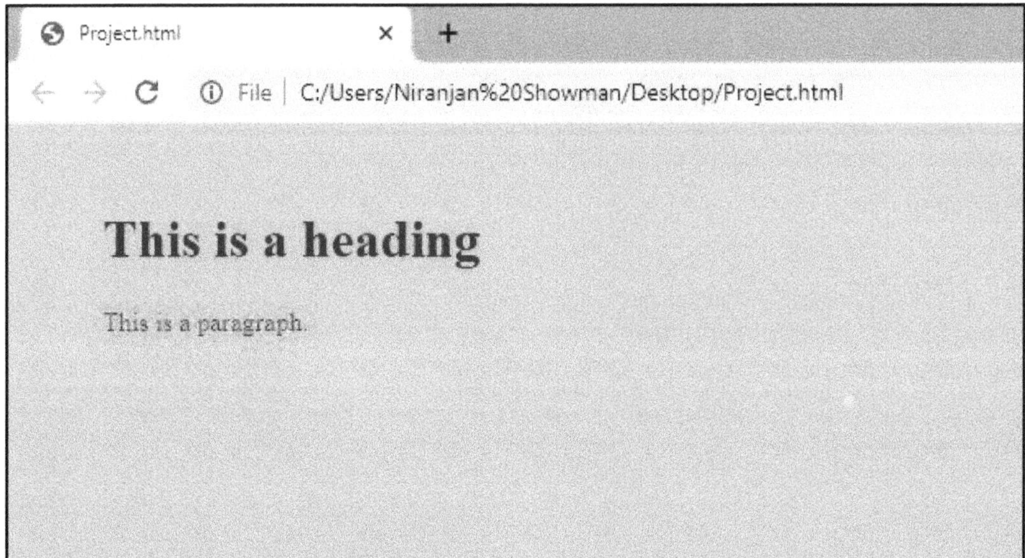

Picture 6.2: The result of Internal CSS.

Project 39 – External CSS

An external style sheet is used to define the style for many HTML pages. To use an external style sheet, add a link to it in the <head> section of each HTML page. For External CSS, you will create two code files, one for HTML, and the other for CSS.

```
<!DOCTYPE html>
<html>
<head>
 <link rel="stylesheet" href="styles.css">
</head>
<body>

<h1>This is a title</h1>
<p>This is a text.</p>

</body>
</html>
```

1. Save this Notepad file on **desktop** with the name: **Project39.html** setting Encoding always as UTF-8.

2. Now you need to write external style sheet in another Notepad file. The file **must not** contain any HTML code, and must be saved with a .css extension.

```
body {
 background-color: purple;
}
h1 {
 color: white;
}
p {

 color: yellow;
}
```

3. Save this CSS file also on **desktop** with the name: **styles.css** setting Encoding always as UTF-8. With an external style sheet, you can change the look of an entire web site, by changing one file.

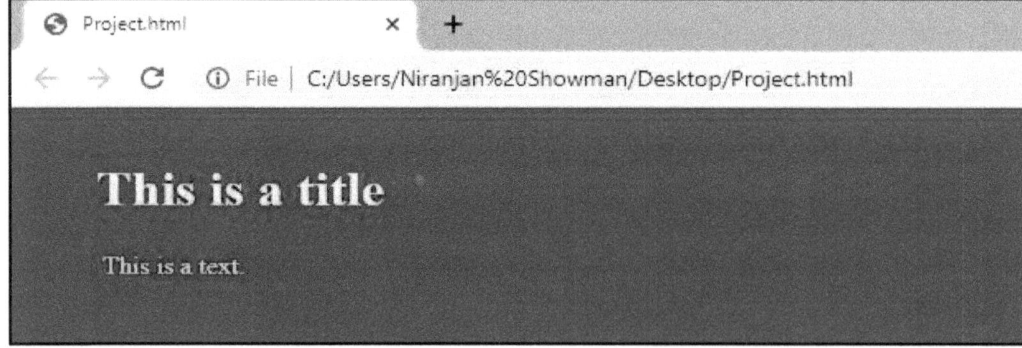

Picture 6.3: The result of External CSS.

Project 40 – CSS Colors, Fonts and Sizes

Here, we will demonstrate some commonly used CSS properties. The CSS **color** property defines the text color to be used. The CSS **font-family** property defines the font to be used. The CSS **font-size** property defines the text size to be used.

```
<!DOCTYPE html>
<html>
<head>
<style>
h1 {
  color: blue;
  font-family: verdana;
  font-size: 300%;

}
p {
  color: red;
  font-family: courier;
  font-size: 160%;
}
</style>
</head>
<body>

<h1>This is a heading</h1>
<p>This is a paragraph.</p>

</body>
</html>
```

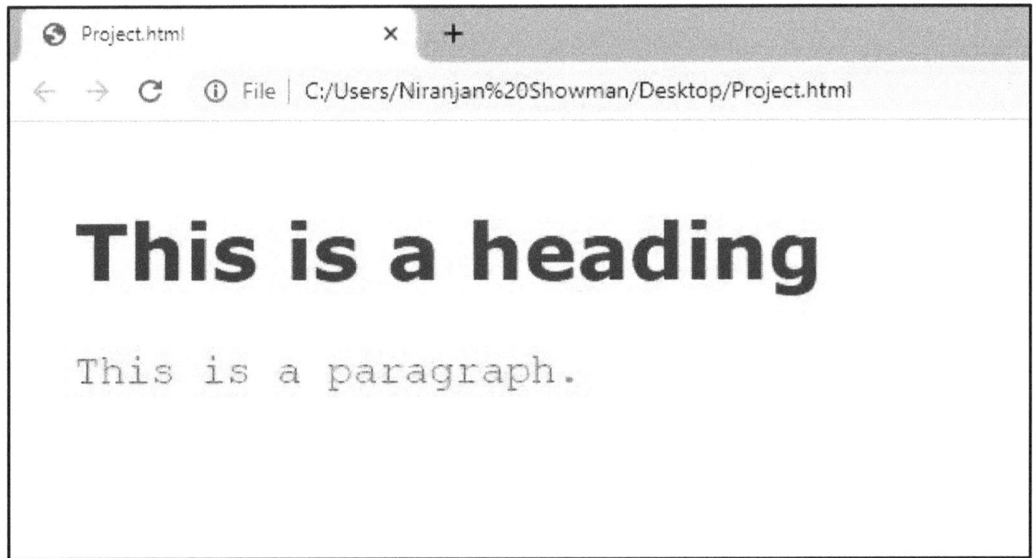

Picture 6.4: The result of CSS colors, fonts and sizes.

Project 41 – CSS Border

The CSS **border** property defines a border around an HTML element. You can define a border for nearly all HTML elements.

```
<!DOCTYPE html>
<html>
<head>

<style>
p {
  border: 2px solid powderblue;
}
</style>
</head>
<body>

<h1>This is a heading</h1>

<p>This is a paragraph.</p>
<p>This is a paragraph.</p>
<p>This is a paragraph.</p>

</body>
</html>
```

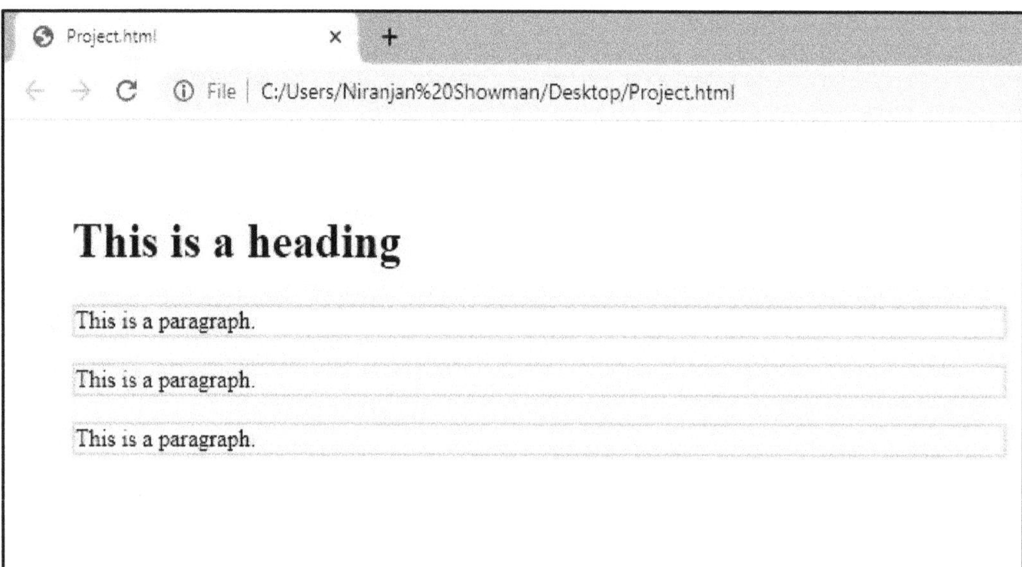

Picture 6.5: The result of CSS border.

You see in the above picture that the CSS border property defines a border around an HTML element. In the subsequent lesson on the next page, you will learn about CSS padding property hat defines a padding (space) between the text and the border.

Project 42 – CSS Padding

The CSS **padding** property defines a padding (space) between the text and the border. Here is the HTML code to apply padding.

```
<!DOCTYPE html>
<html>
<head>

<style>
p {
  border: 2px solid powderblue;
  padding: 30px;
}
</style>
</head>
<body>

<h1>This is a heading</h1>

<p>This is a paragraph.</p>
<p>This is a paragraph.</p>
<p>This is a paragraph.</p>

</body>
</html>
```

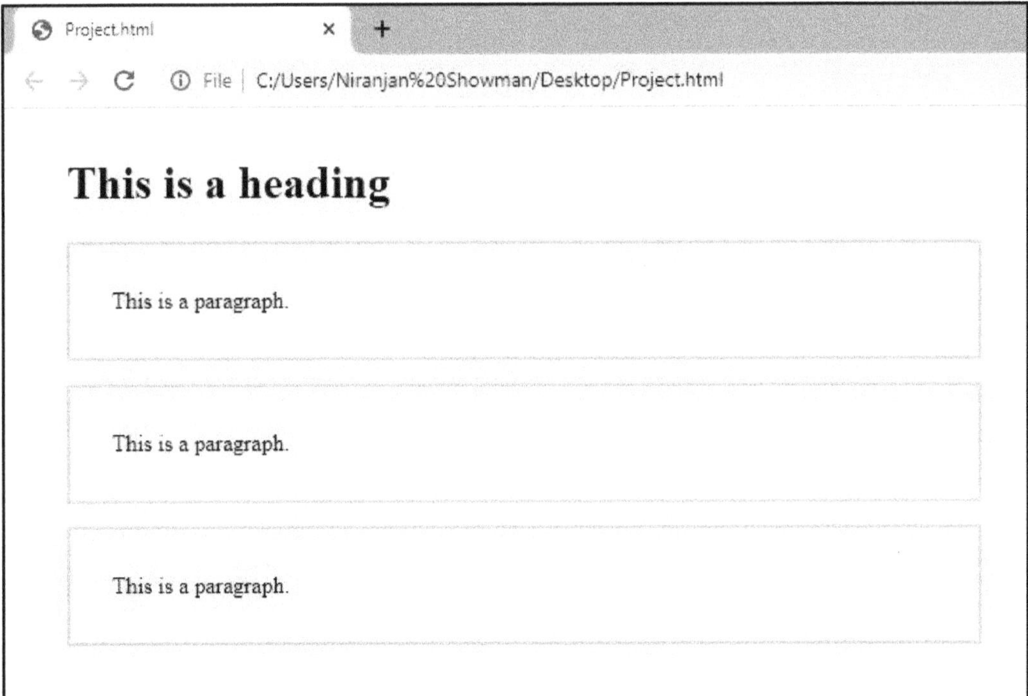

Picture 6.6: The result of CSS padding.

Project 43 – CSS Margin

After border and padding, we are discussing about the CSS **margin** property. This property defines a margin (space) outside the border.

```
<!DOCTYPE html>
<html>
<head>

<style>
p {
  border: 2px solid powderblue;
  margin: 50px;
}
</style>
</head>
<body>

<h1>This is a heading</h1>

<p>This is a paragraph.</p>
<p>This is a paragraph.</p>
<p>This is a paragraph.</p>

</body>
</html>
```

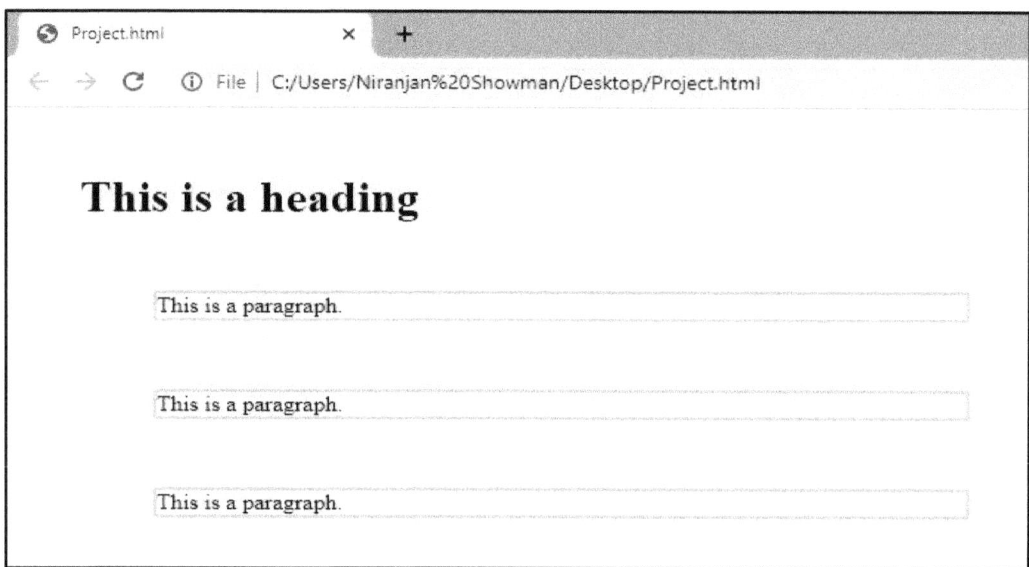

Picture 6.7: The result of CSS margin.

You see in the above picture that the CSS margin property defines a margin (space) outside the border. In the next lesson you will learn about "Clickable Images With Hyperlink".

Project 44 – Clickable Images With Hyperlink

To create an **image hyperlink**, you'll need to use a combination of HTML tags. The primary tags involved are the <img> tag for displaying the image and the <a> tag for creating the hyperlink. Turning web imges into functional links that direct users to other pages is the perfect opportunity for you to enhance navigation and user experience. This functionality can be implemented with the simple HTML tags.

```
<!DOCTYPE html>
<html>
<body>

<h2>Image as a Link</h2>

<p>The image below is a link. Try to click on it.</p>

<a href="https://www.google.com">
<img src="clickit.jpg" width="60" height="40">
</a>

</body>
</html>
```

1. Place an **image file** on your desktop. In my case I have put clickit.jpg.

2. Write the above mentioned code in Notepad and save it as Project44.html also on **desktop**.

3. In **img src** element, write your image file name with **.jpg** extension. JPG and JPEG are the same file format, HTML understands .jpg.

4. When you click the **image hyperlink** of your webpage, it will open **Google.com**.

Picture 6.8: The result of image hyperlink.

Project 45 – Button as a Link

To use an HTML **button** as a link, you have to add some JavaScript code. JavaScript allows you to specify what happens at certain events, such as a click of a button.

```
<!DOCTYPE html>
<html>
<body>

<h2>Button as a Links</h2>
<p>Click the button to go to Cromosys.</p>

<a href="https://www.facebook.com/cromosys">

<button onclick="https://www.facebook.com/cromosys">Cromosys Education</button>

</body>
</html>
```

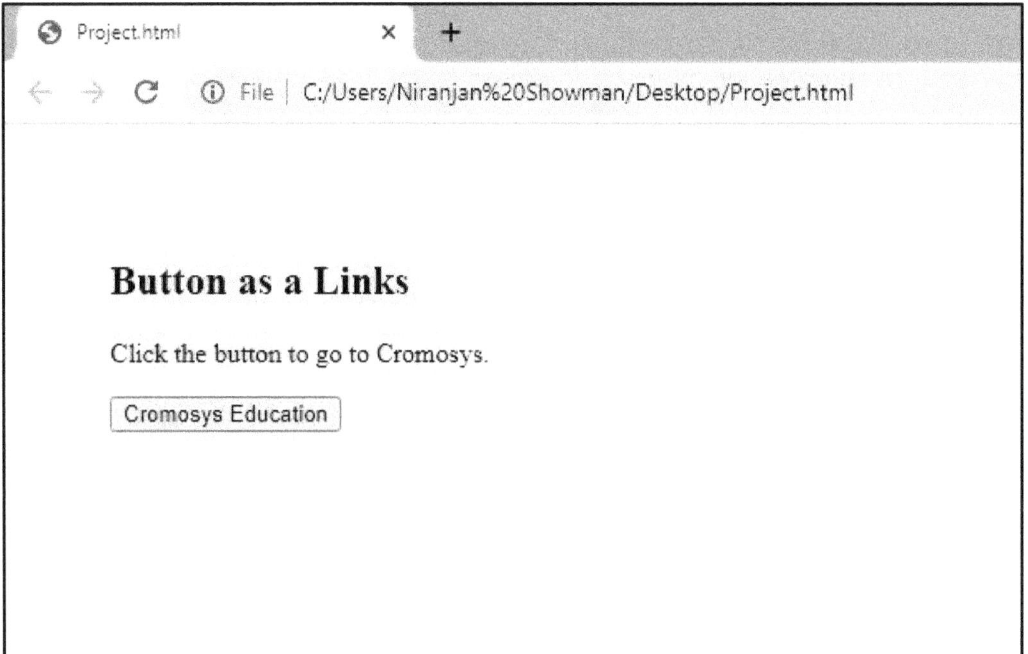

Picture 6.9: The result of button as a link.

In your webpage as shown above, if you click the button **Cromosys Education**, it will open **Facebook.com/cromosys**. We used an HTML button as a link, and we added the JavaScript code. And so JavaScript allows you to specify what happens at certain events.

In the next lesson you will learn about JavaScript in detail. JavaScript is the Programming Language for the Web and it can update and change both HTML and CSS.

2. Using JavaScript

JavaScript is the Programming Language for the Web and it can update and change both HTML and CSS. JavaScript can calculate, manipulate and validate data. It is a scripting or programming language that allows you to implement complex features on web pages. It is a versatile, dynamically typed programming language used for interactive web applications, supporting both client-side and server-side development, and integrating seamlessly with HTML, CSS, and a rich standard library. With JavaScript , every time a web page does more than just sit there and display static information for you to look at. Using JavaScript, web pages display timely content updates, interactive maps, animated 2D/3D graphics, scrolling video jukeboxes, etc. It is the third layer of the layer cake of standard web technologies, two of which (HTML and CSS) we have covered in much more detail.

Project 46 – HTML JavaScript

JavaScript makes HTML pages more dynamic and interactive. This programming language for the web is a single-threaded language that executes one task at a time. It is an Interpreted language which means it executes the code line by line. The code below creates a button on your webpage to show current date and time when you click it.

```
<!DOCTYPE html>
<html>
<body>

<h1>My First JavaScript</h1>

<button type="button"
onclick="document.getElementById('demo').innerHTML = Date()">
Click me to display Date and Time.</button>

<p id="demo"></p>

</body>
</html>
```

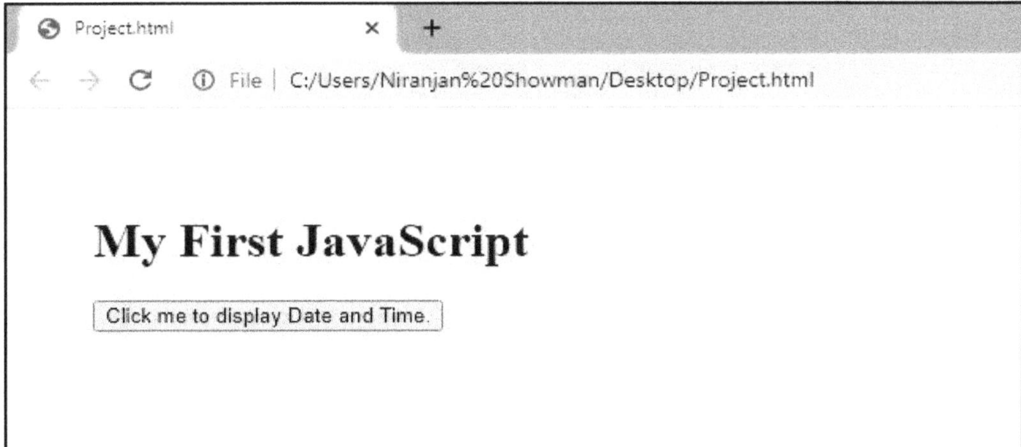

Picture 6.10: The result of JavaScript date and time button.

Project 47 – JavaScript Changing Content

JavaScript can change the content of the webpage. The JavaScript <script> tag is used to define a client-side script. The <script> element either contains script statements, or it points to an external script file through the **src** attribute.

```
<!DOCTYPE html>
<html>
<body>

<h1>My First JavaScript</h1>

<p>JavaScript can change the content of an HTML element:</p>

<button type="button" onclick="myFunction()">Click Me!</button>

<p id="demo">This is a demonstration.</p>

<script>
function myFunction() {
  document.getElementById("demo").innerHTML = "Hello JavaScript!";
}
</script>

</body>
</html>
```

Picture 6.11: The result of JavaScript changing content.

On your result webpage, when you click on "Click Me!" button, it will change the text: **This is a demonstration** into: Hello JavaScript! The JavaScript functions are defined with the function keyword. You can use a function declaration or a function expression.

Project 48 – JavaScript Changing Style

JavaScript can also change the style of an HTML element. Here is the script to change the style when you click the "button" on your webpage.

```
<!DOCTYPE html>
<html>
<body>

<h1>My First JavaScript</h1>

<p id="demo">JavaScript can change the style of an HTML element.</p>

<script>
function myFunction() {
  document.getElementById("demo").style.fontSize = "25px";
  document.getElementById("demo").style.color = "red";
  document.getElementById("demo").style.backgroundColor = "yellow";
}
</script>

<button type="button" onclick="myFunction()">Click Me!</button>

</body>
</html>
```

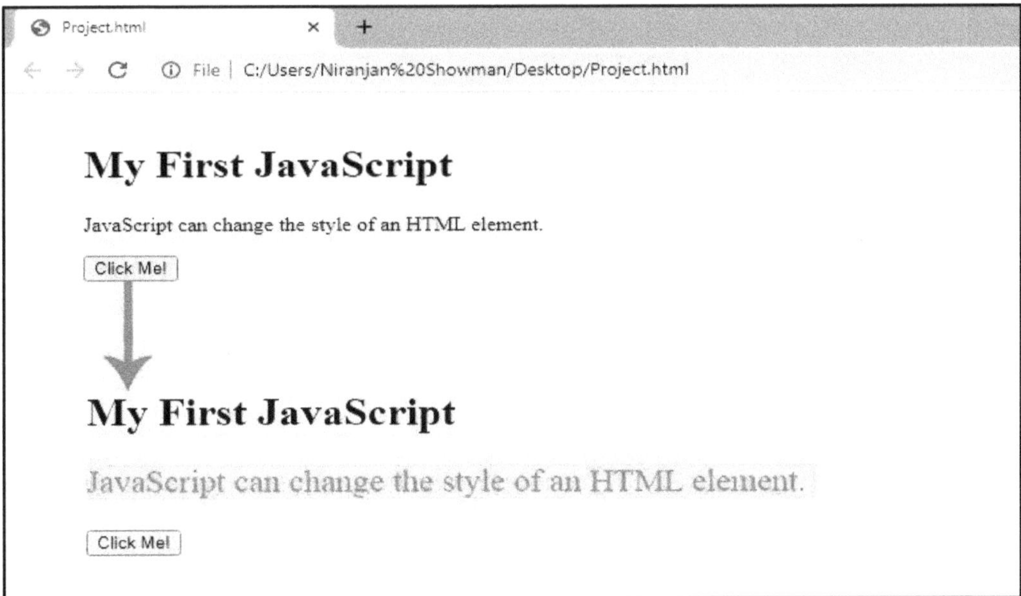

Picture 6.12: The result of JavaScript changing style.

On your result webpage, when you click on "Click Me!" button, it will change the text: **JavaScript can change the style of an HTML element** into: JavaScript can change the style of an HTML element.

JavaScript changes the value of the src (source) attribute of an image. On you result page, you can **switch on** and **switch off** the bulb image by clicking the buttons.

```
<!DOCTYPE html>
<html>
<body>

<h1>My First JavaScript</h1>
<p>Here, a JavaScript changes the value of the src (source) attribute of an image.</p>

<script>
function light(sw) {
 var pic;
 if (sw == 0) {
   pic = "pic_bulboff.gif"
 } else {
   pic = "pic_bulbon.gif"
 }
 document.getElementById('myImage').src = pic;
}
</script>

<img id="myImage" src="pic_bulboff.gif" width="100" height="180">

<p>
<button type="button" onclick="light(1)">Light On</button>
<button type="button" onclick="light(0)">Light Off</button>
</p>

</body>
</html>
```

1. Before writing the code, you need to download two separate images from Internet: (a) **Switched off bulb** and (b) **Switched on blub**, as shown in picture below.

2. Convert these two images into **.gif format** using any online tool and place on your **desktop**.

3. Rename the "off" bulb as: **pic_bulboff**, and "on" bulb as: **pic_bulbon**.

In this code, we have used bulb image of .gif format. GIF images are already widely available on the internet and they are a very common image format used for both static graphics and animated sequences. GIF stands for Graphics Interchange Format.

4. Save this document naming Project49.html on your **desktop**.

5. Now open this document in your browser. Clicking the "Light On" and "Light Off" button, you can see the blub going on and off.

Picture 6.13: The result of JavaScript changing image attribute.

3. Using Emojis in HTML

Emojis are characters from the UTF-8 character set: 😁 😊 ❤. Emojis look like images, or icons, but they are not. They are letters (characters) from the UTF-8 (Unicode) character set. UTF-8 covers almost all of the characters and symbols in the world.

To display an HTML page correctly, a web browser must know the character set used in the page. Emojis are also characters from the UTF-8 alphabet, and they can be copied, displayed, and sized just like any other character in HTML.

😁 is 128516
😊 is 128525
❤ is 128151

Emoji	Value
	🗻
	🗼
	🗽
	🗾
	🗿
	😀
	😁
	😂
	😃
	😄
	😅

Picture 6.14: List of emojis with values.

Project 50 – Using Emojis in HTML

Emojis are characters from the UTF-8 character set. We can use them in HTML mentioning their vlues. To display an HTML page correctly, a web browser must know the character set used in the page.

```
<!DOCTYPE html>
<html>
<meta charset="UTF-8">
<body>

<h1>Sized Emojis</h1>

<p style="font-size:48px">
&#128512; &#128516; &#128525; &#128151;
</p>

</body>
</html>
```

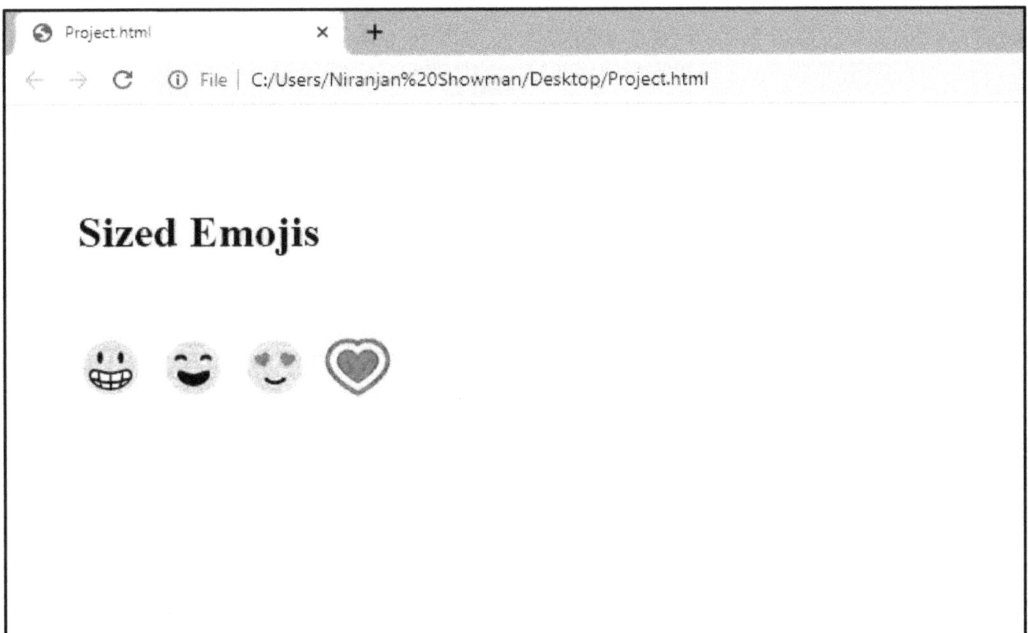

Picture 6.15: The result of emojis in HTML.

Cromosys Publication

Teach Yourself HTML5

Niranjan Jha Showman

NIRANJAN JHA SHOWMAN

Founder - Niranjan Jha Showman

Education and Technology Research Center

Patankar Park, Nallasopara (W), Mumbai. +91-9561450045

Education, Technology, Publication, Healthcare, Newsmedia, Realtor, Filmmaking

www.facebook.com/cromosys

Cromosys Publication
Teach
Yourself
German
NIRANJAN JHA SHOWMAN

Cromosys Publication
Teach Yourself French
NIRANJAN JHA SHOWMAN

Cromosys Publication
Teach
Yourself
Spanish
NIRANJAN JHA SHOWMAN

Cromosys Publication

English
Voice
Accent and
Pronunciation

NIRANJAN JHA SHOWMAN

Teach
Yourself
Autodesk
MAYA
Cromosys Publication
NIRANJAN JHA SHOWMAN

Cromosys Publication
Teach
Yourself
Autodesk
3ds Max
NIRANJAN JHA SHOWMAN

Cromosys Publication
CRIMINAL FACTORY
NIRANJAN JHA SHOWMAN

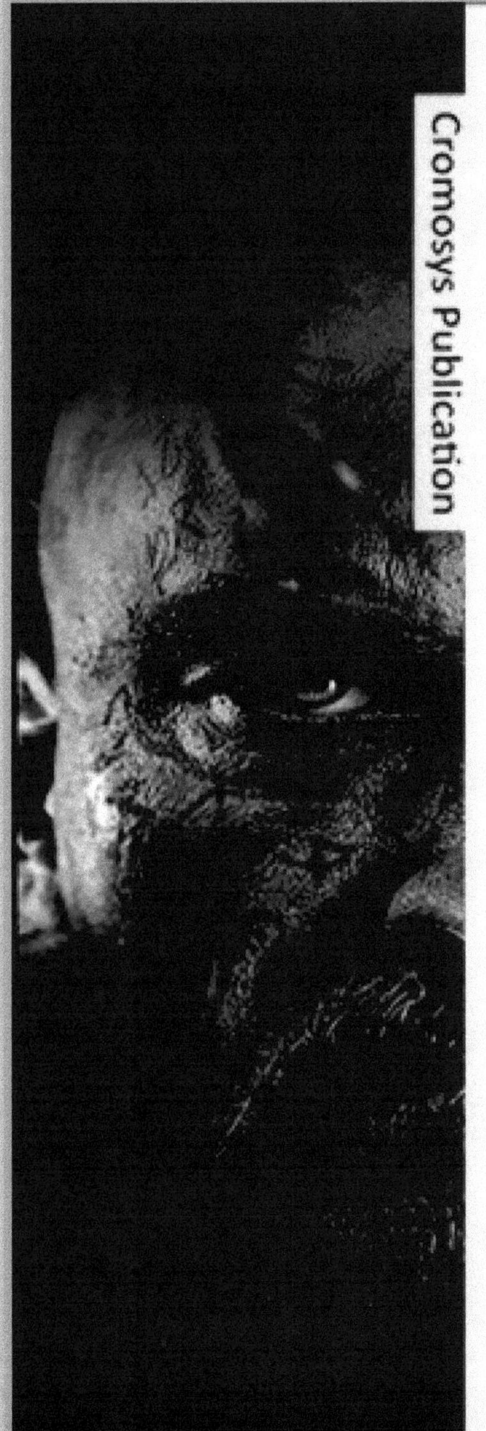

Cromosys Publication
FOCAL DISASTER
NIRANJAN JHA SHOWMAN

Cromosys Publication
Your talents will not help you succeed without your skill of using them.
NIRANJAN JHA SHOWMAN
BE
MILLIONAIRE
LIKE
ME

Cromosys Publication

Teach
Yourself
HTML5

NIRANJAN JHA SHOWMAN